Armar
Yo
to me.
between us, know that you have
made a diffence in my life.

JESUS

First Gift, Then Example

Just thinking of you and Ariana
brings me joy.
  Maybe there will come a
time when you will find
something in this book that
you can connect with. Jesus
has so much love for you.
  Love and blessings,
  David Dorries

JESUS

First Gift, Then Example

David W. Dorries, Ph.D.

Copyright © 2018 David W. Dorries, Ph.D.

All rights reserved.

ISBN:1720509328

ISBN-13:978-1720509325

CreateSpace Independent Publishing Platform
North Charleston, South Carolina

TABLE OF CONTENTS

Dedication……………………………..……...v

Introduction………………….…..……....vii

Chapter 1 – Jesus Is First Gift.…...………………...1

Chapter 2 - The Challenge of Pelagianism…….......9

Chapter 3 - The Challenge of Semi-Pelagianism ...20

Chapter 4 - Semi-Pelagianism and Conversion 27

Chapter 5 - Semi-Pelagianism and Sanctification...35

Chapter 6 - Semi-Pelagianism to the Present Day..46

Chapter 7 - Jesus Modeled Spirit Dependency…...61

Chapter 8 - Jesus: Baptizer in the Holy Spirit….....74

Chapter 9 - Jesus: Receiver of the Spirit……...…..82

Chapter 10 - Jesus: Empowerment………………..94

Chapter 11 - Jesus: Speaking in Tongues……......108

Chapter 12 – Conclusion……………...…….....137

APPENDIX I..151
APPENDIX II..154

DEDICATION

To Martha Whitten,

My Sister and Hero,

Whose life of surrender to God's grace

Is a modern-day testament of the love of Jesus

INTRODUCTION

IN THE 1990'S, A GRASSROOTS MOVEMENT arose among Christian young people in the United States in which teenagers wore wrist bands displaying the letters WWJD. This acronym posed the question, "What would Jesus do?" Awareness was raised to consider how Jesus might have responded and to follow His example in the contemporary situations of daily life.

This was not the first major emphasis within the Christian world to address the topic of following Jesus' example. In 1896, Charles Sheldon published a novel that gained widespread attention entitled, *In His Steps*. The subtitle of his book was, *What Would Jesus Do?* Going even further back, a Catholic monk from the Modern Devotion movement, Thomas a Kempis, wrote a book entitled, *The Imitation of Christ*. The popularity of this book has been immense. Originally published sometime between 1418 and 1427, *The Imitation of Christ* has been published into more languages than any religious book other than the Bible. The book is a sobering and soul-searching appeal to emulate Christ's life of suffering and self-denial.

The theme of Jesus Christ being our example is reflected in the title of this book, *Jesus: First Gift, Then Example*. I did not coin this statement. Credit goes to Martin Luther, 16th century Protestant Reformer.[1] Yet his approach was anything but an endorsement of calls for emulating Jesus' lifestyle. He insisted that a prior step, i.e., receiving Jesus as Gift, was essential before any consideration could be given to emulating the life and teachings of Christ. Luther recognized a symptom that no one else seemed to recognize. All human beings have a sin problem, and until the Biblical remedy is properly applied, all religious effort and good works are futile. Nothing could be more pretentious than attempting to live according to the lifestyle of Jesus without first receiving Him as Gift!

---

[1] Weimar Edition, W, 10/I/2, 247, quoted I.D.K. Siggins, *Martin Luther's Doctrine of Christ*, New Haven: Yale University Press, 1970, p. 159.

Luther's approach to justification represented a paradigm shift in the contemporary landscape of his day. The finished work of Jesus Christ brought an end to all roads to right standing with God except one. "For God so loved the world that **He gave** His only begotten Son ..." (John 3:16) Receiving Him as a Gift brings the complete transformation of human nature, resulting in Jesus Himself indwelling the believer through the living presence of the Holy Spirit. The meaning of the words of the Apostle Paul come alive in this context. "I have been crucified with Christ; and it is no longer I who live, but Christ lives in me; ..." (Galatians 2:20)

Following Jesus as example, in Luther's time and ours, can have meaning only when understood within the dynamic of the crucified, risen and ascended Christ coming to dwell inside the believer through the Holy Spirit purely as a Gift of God's grace. Now, the issue is not trying to live as Jesus lived and trying to obey His teachings. Our agenda now is responding to the living Christ who dwells within us. Hebrews 13:8 reveals that "Jesus Christ is the same yesterday, today and forever." We don't attempt to emulate the lifestyle of a dead hero. We daily allow His cross to mortify our self-life so that the living Jesus can have the freedom to be Lord of our thoughts, words and deeds.

Let's get back to the WWJD movement of the 90's. Although well-intentioned, I think we now can see that such an emphasis can lead to a performance-oriented agenda leaving adherents on an endless treadmill of striving and disappointment. Perhaps a little tweaking of the acronym would shed light on the problem. Changing one letter makes a world of difference. WIJD captures the paradigm shift of emphasis. Not, What Would Jesus Do? Instead, **What Is Jesus Doing?**[2] Attention is now placed upon the living Jesus dwelling within us. As we respond to His initiative, He is free to direct our lives. Renewing our mind through the Biblical revelation facilitates the Holy Spirit's task of imparting His living presence into every fiber of our being. Receiving Jesus first as Gift changes everything. We are dead to self-life and have been transformed into a Temple of the Holy Spirit. Instead of us performing for Him, Jesus is now the Performer, inhabiting us and living through us in all the fullness of who He is. This truth transformed Christianity in Luther's day, leading to a Reformation. This truth holds the same potential to birth a New Reformation in our day! May this book help to awaken us to that end.

---

[2] My first exposure to the idea of replacing WWJD with WIJD came for a discussion with a dear friend and former colleague, Dr. Daniel Thimell.

Chapter 1

Jesus is First Gift

Luther's Insight

AS NOTED IN THE INTRODUCTION, sixteenth century Protestant Reformer Martin Luther identified Jesus as "first gift, then example." He was calling attention to the futility of attempting to follow the example of Jesus' lifestyle without having first received Him as gift. Jesus lived His life as a model of human virtue and fulfillment, but His example is completely unattainable where sin dominates the human condition. Therefore, Jesus' exemplary role is secondary to His redemptive purpose. Only because Jesus was successful in the fulfillment of His redemptive mission is it possible for Adam's race to emulate Jesus' lifestyle. Redemption became possible when Jesus rose triumphantly from the grave and breathed upon His disciples to receive the Holy Spirit (John 20:22). Since that time, salvation has been available for all people who are willing to receive Jesus as Savior.[3] Only those recipients, i.e., the company of redeemed humanity, are in a position to live according to Jesus' example. The Holy

---

[3] Scholars disagree as to when the new birth became available to believers. I hold that Jesus imparted regeneration in His John 20:22 appearance on the night of His resurrection. Now in His glorified body, meeting with His followers for the first time since His finished work of redemption had been won on Calvary's cross, He breathed upon His disciples and commanded them to receive the Holy Spirit. As He breathed on them the restoration of *zoe* life lost to humanity since Adam's fall, Jesus was re-enacting the breath of *zoe* life breathed into humanity at Creation (Genesis 2:7). Some scholars contend that the new birth could not have occurred until the Day of Pentecost, when Jesus baptized His followers with the Holy Spirit. (See Dr. Betty Gilliam's treatment in this regard in her excellent book, *Introduction to Holy Spirit: The Faith Connection,* CreateSpace, 2018, pp. 183-195). I believe that Pentecost was a logically distinct impartation of the Spirit for ministry empowerment rather than the new birth. John 7:39 is the most problematic verse for my position. The context of this verse is during Jesus' public ministry. John explains that "the Spirit was not yet given, because Jesus was not yet glorified." Most would contend that Jesus' glorification occurred at His Ascension, when He was raised to the Right Hand of the Father. In that case, if the Spirit was not yet given until after His ascension, then the new birth of regeneration could not have occurred on the night of Jesus' resurrection when He breathed on the disciples. I would wish to add, however, that Jesus' glorification was more of a process that culminated in His Ascension. On the night of Jesus' arrest and on the eve of His Crucifixion, as He agonized in prayer in the Garden, He told His disciples, "The hour has come for the Son of Man to be glorified." His death on the Cross certainly was the beginning of His glorification. As the Risen Lord in His glorified body, what would prevent Him from having the authority to impart the new birth to His disciples? This view allows for a clear distinction between the Spirit's work of regeneration and the Spirit's baptism of empowerment which occurred later at Pentecost. However, this lengthy commentary has little bearing upon our text. Whether the new birth occurred on the night of His resurrection or on the Day of Pentecost, salvation and eternal life have been available ever since for all who believe!

Spirit that Jesus imparts to every believer provides the enabling power to follow Jesus' example of abundant living. Humanity devoid of the Holy Spirit is powerless to emulate the lifestyle Jesus modeled.

Recovery of the Gospel's Liberating Power

Luther's insight, that Jesus is "first gift, then example," provided a necessary critique to late Medieval Catholicism's burdensome system of conditional standards of human performance required for salvation. Luther sought to educate people concerning the priority of receiving Jesus as gift, thus eliminating performance as a condition for salvation. Luther's discovery restored to the Gospel its liberating power, and reestablished salvation as a gift of God's grace. Most of all, it exalted Jesus in His rightful place as God's "indescribable gift!" (II Corinthians 9:15)

Human Helplessness and God's Love

The biblical doctrine of salvation is logically founded upon the premise that Jesus is gift. The most basic salvation passage in the Bible affirms this. "For God so loved the world, that **He gave** His only begotten Son, that whoever believes in Him should not perish, but have eternal life." (John 3:16) God, in His tripartite being as Father, Son and Spirit, is pure love. The plan of salvation was born in the heart of God. God, motivated by compassion for the sinful, alienated race of humanity, designed and implemented a plan whereby His creatures could be redeemed and restored to relationship with Himself. The salvation of humanity is solely an accomplishment of God, and is a result of His love, mercy and grace. The opportunity for salvation became a reality when humanity was absolutely helpless. No prerequisites or qualifications on the human side were taken into account in the origination of God's plan. By its very nature, salvation is a gift from God to the human race.

Gracious Alternative

Rather than separate Himself eternally from His fallen creatures, God exercised His mercy. He chose to provide a gracious alternative to the punishment and judgment deserved by every creature. Not that He would simply overlook the reality of sin and its consequences. His justice required that sin be punished and judged. But love motivated Him to bear the full consequences of sin upon Himself, so that He might extend pardon and life to those who deserved His judgment.

Gracious Exchange

By definition, "grace" means **unmerited favor**. Salvation has its source in God's grace, apart from any consideration of merit on the part of potential recipients. Jesus, God's Son, came into the very place where sin abounded, taking into His own person the human nature entrapped by sin, bringing reconciliation and righteousness into the arena formerly under sin's control. Jesus, in His own person, abolished the wall of sin dividing Holy God from sinful humanity. He substituted obedience for disobedience, thus healing the humanity that sin had dominated by removing its condemnation. He also substituted His own freedom from suffering and judgment due to His sinlessness for the punishment sinful humanity deserved. As the apostle Paul clarifies, "He made Him who knew no sin to be sin on our behalf, that we might become the righteousness of God in Him." (II Corinthians 5:21) This gracious exchange, enacted by Jesus, is the basis of human salvation.

Faith: Acceptance of the Gift

No biblical passage better describes the dynamics of salvation, with its characteristic emphasis upon the graciousness of God coupled with the helplessness of humanity, than a segment of Paul's letter to the Ephesians. "For by grace you have been saved through faith; and that not of yourselves, it is the gift of God; not as a result of works, that no one should boast." (Ephesians 2:8-9) Paul tells the Ephesian Christians that their salvation is a result of God's graciousness. For salvation to become actualized for the individual, it must be appropriated by faith. Faith is simply the individual's acceptance of the gift of salvation. Faith is the means of transmission, whereby salvation is conveyed from God to humanity. Faith conveys specifically to the individual the salvation won by Jesus generally for all humankind.

Faith is Not a Work

Paul wants to be sure that the reader does not confuse the faith that appropriates salvation with a human work considered necessary to be performed in exchange for salvation. If any work, even faith, is regarded as a human requirement for salvation, then salvation ceases to be a gift and can no longer be attributed to the graciousness of God. Earlier in his Ephesian letter, Paul extols the blessings coming to the believer through Jesus' redemption, ascribing it "to the praise of the glory of His grace, which He freely bestowed on us in the Beloved." (Ephesians 1:6) The faith to receive Jesus and His salvation must never be considered a work on our part, something done to earn our salvation. That would leave room on our part for boasting that we had contributed to our own salvation. Paul approves of boasting only in God, whose graciousness solely is responsible for our salvation. "And what do you have that you did not receive? But if you did receive it, why do you boast as if you had not received it?" (I Corinthians 4:7)

Luther's Personal Pilgrimage

Martin Luther's sixteenth century rediscovery of these basic biblical truths, allowing him to conclude that Jesus is "first gift" before He can be viewed in any sense as an example for human behavior, came to him after years of personal struggle. Luther's personal theological pilgrimage led him to a fresh understanding of the Pauline doctrine of "justification." Justification relates to "the state of being made right by God." Justification is not a determination of humanity. Only God has the prerogative to justify. Luther rightly saw himself as a sinner, condemned by God and deserving to spend eternity in hell. A product of late Medieval Catholicism, Luther sought justification with God through the prescribed avenues of conduct set before him. He sought to live a holy, penitent life. Yet his conscience tormented him. He was aware of evil motives behind even his best behavior and found no escape from the anger and wrath of God.

Luther's Breakthrough

A crisis experience during his university years led Luther to a drastic conclusion. He decided to enter a monastery and become a monk and priest. He reasoned that the way to justification would not be denied him if he dedicated himself to a lifetime of monastic devotion. Yet years of religious achievement did not move him any closer to salving his troubled conscience before God. Luther's breakthrough eventuated as he undertook teaching duties at the University of Wittenberg. As Bible lecturer, Luther became immersed in scriptural study, climaxing in personal theological discovery of God's grace revealed in Jesus. Luther's sense of sinfulness was swept away as he recognized justification as a gift of God's grace won by Jesus' righteousness, and without any works or merits on the part of humanity. As Luther centered his life and ministry upon the theme of "justification by grace through faith," and the practical implications of this doctrine in the church, a Reformation was born that completely altered the course of Western civilization.

Recovery of Augustine

Luther concluded that all efforts to live a virtuous and religious life after the pattern of Jesus are futile without first receiving Jesus as the gift of God's grace. Good works are not the **root** of righteousness, but the **fruit** of a life inhabited by Jesus though the Holy Spirit. Yet Luther did not claim originality in his "reformation discovery." He saw himself merely as a product of a rich biblical heritage, epitomized by the Apostle Paul's definitive teachings concerning our justification by grace. Luther was also a product of the teachings of perhaps the most influential of the Western Church Fathers, Saint Augustine. Known as the "Church Father of God's Grace," Augustine helped revive the fifth century church with a fresh understanding of "justification by grace" when threatened by the Pelagian heresy. As an Augustinian monk, Luther was familiar with Augustine's writings and keenly aware of the issues at stake in the Augustinian-Pelagian controversy. A careful look at this ancient controversy not only will shed additional light on Luther's Reformation discovery, but also will accentuate our exploration of the identity of Jesus. Our awareness will be deepened in the truth that Jesus is God's "indescribable gift!"

Chapter 2

Jesus as Gift: The Challenge of Pelagianism

THE GOSPEL OF OUR LORD JESUS CHRIST is "good news" precisely because the redemption that Jesus purchased for humanity is a free gift. Redemption is available to all persons and cannot be earned or merited. Although all are sinners, all who receive the gift of God's grace in Christ automatically are considered by the Father to be righteous. No amount of personal works by the sinner can attain righteousness. Receiving Jesus allows righteousness to be transferred as a gift to the believer's account. This glorious truth is the only means for human salvation and represents the very essence of the Christian Gospel. Historically, the most direct challenge to the truth of the Gospel, i.e., that redemption is a free gift in Jesus Christ, was contrived by Pelagius in the fifth century. He remains the archenemy of the grace of God.

The Rise of Pelagianism

Pelagius (360-431) was a British monk who visited Rome early in the fifth century. Pelagius was shocked at the expression of Christianity that he witnessed in Rome, being alarmed particularly by what he judged to be the declining moral standards of the church. He traced the root of the problem to what he believed to be a state of "theological passivity" among Christians, spawned by the teachings of none other than the influential bishop of Hippo, North Africa, St. Augustine. Pelagius viewed Augustine's emphasis upon God's sovereignty as promoting a passive fatalism among believers, leading to moral indifference. Pelagius saw it as his place to provide the church with an alternative to Augustinianism. He developed a doctrinal stance in contrast to Augustine and attracted a band of proselytes who traveled with him to spread this novel teaching.

Salvation by Works

Pelagius assumed that the best way to encourage the church to embrace a strict moral standard is to emphasize human responsibility in the salvation process. He taught that the Mosiac Law was an obtainable standard of human behavior, even without God's provision of redemption accomplished by Jesus. He considered it to be an absurd contention that God would have commanded His people to obey laws that were impossible for them to keep. He believed that numerous biblical characters, both from the Old and New Testaments, lived without sin and therefore gained salvation as a result of their own obedience to the

Law. Pelagius concluded that we can assume that when sin is not mentioned in connection with Biblical characters that they were sinless, e.g., Abel, Enoch, Daniel, Deborah, Mary (the mother of Jesus), etc. Such teaching, of course, ignores the doctrine of original sin and contradicts Paul's assertion that "all have sinned and fall short of the glory of God." (Romans 3:23)

Even more dangerous is Pelagius' belief that salvation can be obtained without Jesus and His redemptive triumph. Pelagius did not deny Jesus' work on the cross and His resurrection, but viewed the redemption won by Jesus as a "secondary grace" to be utilized only if sin is committed. Jesus comes into the Pelagian picture only when sin is committed. His grace is available to provide forgiveness and restoration. Once the sinner is restored, Jesus fades out of the picture. Righteousness remains a matter of one's adherence to the Law. In the final analysis, God's verdict of righteousness is based upon the righteous deeds of the believer, not by faith in Jesus' righteousness.

"Primary Grace" is Free Will

Pelagius presupposed that all humans are created good, based upon the "primary grace" of free will every person receives when they are conceived. Having evidence of God's grace in the functional capacity to freely choose, every person is expected by God to live in perfection according to His holy Law. Every person is born in a state of neutrality, just as with Adam and Eve before they sinned. Pelagius denied that the sin of Adam and Eve resulted in a "fall" of the human race. Since no "fall" occurred, the descendants of Adam and Eve did not inherit "original sin" or a "sin nature." The first sin in the Garden was an isolated act. Every person approaches each new circumstance with a clean slate, just as Adam and Eve faced the choice of eating the forbidden fruit without proclivity to sin. God expects total obedience. When sin is chosen, the "secondary grace" of Jesus is brought into play. Once forgiveness is obtained, restoring neutrality, the cycle begins again. Jesus is set aside, and the individual returns to dependence upon the "primary grace" of one's own free will. In the end, the goal of Pelagianism is a lifetime of unbroken righteous actions that ultimately gain promotion to heaven.

Pelagianism Condemned at the Council of Ephesus (431)
Pelagius proved to be an elusive nemesis for the fifth century church. He stayed on the run. Remaining in one location only long enough to plant a small cadre of adherents, and, as opposition surfaced, escaping before he could be apprehended, only to plant another seed of heresy elsewhere, Pelagius dotted the landscape with pockets of festering doctrinal disease that troubled Christendom for a season.

Recognizing the danger lurking beneath the disguise of Pelagius' apparent "moral revolution," Augustine was the leading authority in the church's refutation and repression of the Pelagian heresy. Augustine's compelling and brilliantly insightful writings against Pelagianism brought to the surface the erroneous nature of this movement, discrediting its appeal. A year after Augustine's death, as the bishops of the church convened at the Council of Ephesus in 431, Pelagianism was officially condemned. Pelagianism in its ancient doctrinal formulation ceased to be a serious threat to the Gospel of Jesus Christ.

Augustine's Refutation

Augustine's refutation of Pelagianism refreshed the fifth century church with the priority and absolute necessity of God's grace in Jesus for the salvation of humankind. Augustine taught that an actual "fall" occurred in the Garden of Eden, separating a holy and loving God from His sinful creatures. Adam's fall into sin altered the nature of humanity. Adam's original nature was inclined towards the good. With Adam's sin came the fall of the human race. Adam and all his posterity became infected with "original sin" and hereditary guilt. Human nature after the fall is inclined towards evil. All of humanity, therefore, stands under the judgment of God, for the sinful nature inherited by all inevitably results in the committing of actual sins against God. For Augustine, sinful humanity is faced with an irresolvable dilemma with no way of escape.

Gratia Christi

Since humanity was helplessly alienated from Creator God, the only possible remedy must come from God

Himself. Augustine taught that human sin did not stop God's love for His fallen creatures. God responded to fallen humanity by exercising His grace. He enacted a plan of salvation, involving the costly sacrifice of His own Son as an offering for the sins of the people. Augustine linked God's grace with the gift of Jesus Christ (*gratia Christi*). Without the gracious gift of His Son, Jesus, there is no possibility for human salvation.

Salvation is God's Work of Grace

Augustine contended that no ethical or religious behavior on the part of humanity could earn right standing with God. Even the faith to believe in Jesus' redemption is a product of God's grace and is not to be viewed as an independent work of merit deserving God's favor. In human salvation, the initiative always comes from God. Humanity can only respond. All glory and credit, therefore belongs to God.

Grace from Start to Finish

From Augustine's perspective, God's grace works progressively in the human condition. Within the family of God, children are presented for baptism. The seed of Jesus is imparted to the infant, beginning a journey of progressive transformation through God's gracious initiative. Outside the church, the conversion process begins with **prevenient grace**, as the Holy Spirit draws the individual to the knowledge of Jesus. A longing for redemption is imparted. Next, **operational grace** creates faith in the individual, resulting in a union between Jesus and the human soul. **Cooperational grace** does its work of transforming and emancipating the human will to bring forth fruits of faith. **Perfecting grace** produces perseverance in the individual, leading to eternal life and the perfect state. The work of perfecting grace does not reach completion until the believer is resurrected with Jesus. Augustine viewed salvation as a process, with God's grace involved at every level from start to finish.

Pelagianism: Moral Perfectionism

Augustine's explication of salvation, involving God's gracious initiative through Jesus on every level, served to uproot the shaky foundations of Pelagian doctrine. The most serious, dangerous error of the Pelagian system is to deny the necessity of human salvation through the gift of Jesus Christ. If God's grace was imparted at creation, endowing humanity with the ability to live righteously and earn eternal life, then the Gospel itself and the costly sacrifice of Jesus Christ is rendered unnecessary. If Jesus' saving work is reduced to nothing more than a roadside recovery for those who temporarily falter in life's journey, but the final reward at the end of the line is a product of human moral achievement, then the Gospel itself has been jettisoned and replaced by a humanistic system of moral perfectionism.

Pelagian Jesus: Assists in Self-Help

Pelagianism contends that the goal of human life is moral perfectionism according to the Mosaic Law of the Old Testament. All persons will be judged according to their adherence to the Law. Eternal life is based upon righteous conduct. The appearance of Jesus in history primarily is to provide forgiveness for those who lapse into sin. His forgiveness does not bring eternal life, but removes the sin, thus restoring the individual to a previous state of neutrality. Complete adherence to the Law remains the basis of eternal life. It must be said that Pelagius allowed for an additional role to be contributed by Jesus. The perfectionism of Jesus' life is meant to inspire emulation and instruction in righteous conduct. In the end, however, eternal life must be merited by righteous works performed by the individual. At best, Jesus' contribution is to assist the individual to attain righteousness. He is not a factor in the final judgment. Everyone must stand or fall according to one's own righteousness.

Justification is Based upon the Righteousness Obtained by Jesus

Augustinianism turned the tables on Pelagianism by asserting that no person can achieve eternal life based upon their own merits of righteousness. Every person stands condemned before God because of sin. The only solution for sinful humanity is God's gracious choice to provide salvation as a free gift through His Son. For those willing to receive salvation through faith, salvation and eternal life are provided freely without merit. Justification with God is not based upon human moral accomplishment, but upon the righteousness attained by Jesus and transferred undeservedly and without merit as a gracious gift to the recipient. Faith in the living Jesus and His redemptive work actualizes the transfer.

The Council of Ephesus (431) Upheld the Gospel

The Council of Ephesus (431) confirmed Augustine's refutation of Pelagianism. The Council officially condemned Pelagius' teachings as heretical. Augustine's writings against Pelagius represent a landmark of defense against any attempt to base the salvation of the Gospel upon any system of ethical and/or religious works. The Christian Gospel must always be founded upon justifcation through the merits of Jesus' righteousness, graciously given without condition to all who receive by faith. We all are sinners and cannot help ourselves. God Himself has made possible our relationship with Him, and Jesus is the door to that relationship. Jesus is God's gracious gift, and our life now and eternally with God is through Him.

Liberal Protestantism: Pelagianism Revisited

The most serious reappearance in Christian history of the Pelagian type of heresy is the Liberal Protestantism that swept across Europe in the nineteenth century. This pervasive movement that sought to reinterpret essential biblical doctrines in accordance with Enlightenment presuppositions displayed striking similarities with the Pelagian worldview. Liberalism denied the reality of "original sin" in the human condition and cast Jesus in the role primarily of inspirational example of the religious and ethical ideal of human achievement. Going beyond Pelagianism, Liberalism denied Jesus' deity and the atoning value of Jesus' shed blood. Pelagius, however, misapplied these facets of orthodoxy, leading him to similar conclusions later embraced by Liberalism. Both movements reduced Jesus' primary role to that of moral/religious example, and robbed Him of His redemptive triumph at Calvary, in that they advocated the inherent moral perfectibility of humanity apart from Jesus' atonement.

Jesus Reduced to the Guru of Self-Help

Liberal Protestantism did a major disservice to Western society at large by attempting to legitimize an unorthodox version of Christianity catering to "modern" sensibilities. The "demythologization" of the Gospel resulted in a "modernized" culture positive about moral and religious perfectibility through educational acquisition. Knowledge is power, and abundant methods of self-help release the vastness of human potential for every person who possesses the will-power to succeed. In this model, Jesus becomes the "guru" of self-help, whose loving and giving lifestyle and willingness to lay down His life for others represents a larger-than-life model for self-giving. Such accommodation permits modern humanity to be moderately religious and altruistic, while steering clear of Gospel essentials such as sin, the Cross, blood atonement, new birth, resurrection, the supernatural, and final judgment.

Chapter 3

Jesus as Gift: The Challenge of Semi-Pelagianism

PREFACING THIS CHAPTER with a brief historical summary of a heresy is not without purpose. Semi-Pelagianism, as it came to be known, followed closely on the heels and is a direct offspring of Pelagianism. Both shared the same threatening characteristic. Each represented an attack upon the foundational Scriptural revelation that Jesus Christ is the supreme gift of God's grace to humanity, and to receive Him as such is the only way to salvation.

Attack on the Giftedness of Salvation

As an historical movement, semi-Pelagianism was short-lived and only regionally influential. As the church gained awareness of the subtle errors contained in this theology, a consensus of bishops decisively condemned the doctrine. Yet as a system of thought, semi-Pelagianism has wormed its way into the presuppositions and beliefs of several generations of Christians throughout history. It parades itself as a doctrine giving due honor and recognition to human responsibility, but its true character is to siphon over into the resume' of human merit some of the glory due to God alone for the gift of Jesus Christ and His salvation, thus compromising the very nature of Christian salvation as a pure gift from a gracious God.

A Variation of Pelagianism

Sympathizers of Pelagius' teachings were formulating a compromise position even before the church's pronouncement of heresy against Pelagianism became official in 431. Pelagius' disregard for the necessity of Jesus' redemptive work in human salvation could not be tolerated, but Pelagian adherents concluded that a subtle variation of this theme held the promise of gaining widespread sympathy.

Last Writings of Augustine

This compromise perspective, initially known as Massilianism and later labeled semi-Pelagianism,[4] made its early headway in southern France. The doctrine had gained enough attention by the early fifth century that news reached Augustine of its existence during the waning years of his life. Finding cause for concern, Augustine managed to pen the final two writings of his illustrious

---

[4] The term, semi-Pelagianism, was not coined until the Scholastic era.

career[5] in an attempt to repel the advancement of this dangerous doctrine.

Augustine's corrective efforts were not enough to slow the growing momentum of semi-Pelagian doctrine, and its influence continued to spread after Augustine's death in 430. Throughout the fifth century, semi-Pelagianism dominated the theology of the French church, yet not without strong resistance from Augustinian sympathizers.[6]

Official Condemnation

Three decades into the sixth century, resistance solidified noticeably, and the bishops rallied together to take official action against this aberrant theology. Convening in 529, the bishops of the Second Council of Orange concluded that the semi-Pelagian doctrine failed to meet the standards of Christian orthodoxy. The Council's refutation involved the formulation of twenty-five articles affirming truths of Scripture and milder aspects of Augustinian theology while repudiating points of semi-Pelagian doctrine. The condemnation of semi-Pelagianism gained

---

[5] *On the Predestination of the Saints* and *On the Gift of Perseverance*, included in *A Select Library of the Nicene and Post-Nicene Fathers of the Christian Church*, ed. Philip Schaff, vol. V (Saint Augustin: Anti-Pelagian Writings), Grand Rapids: Eerdmans Publishing Company, 1956.

[6] Various degrees of adherence to the Augustinian system of doctrine were evident in the movement to resist semi-Pelagianism. The dominant party standing against semi-Pelagianism did not come from sympathizers of Augustine's absolute predestination theory, but rather from moderate Augustinians.

additional support in 530 when the bishop of Rome, Boniface II, ratified the decisions of the Council of Orange. After the Orange proceedings, the movement never really flourished again.

Worldview Has Persisted
Yet semi-Pelagianism as a system of thought did not disappear. At various junctures within Christian history, semi-Pelagian presuppositions have resurfaced to cloud the vision and distort the way for generations of Christians. Our task through the remainder of this chapter will be to identify the basic presuppositions of semi-Pelagianism, expose its doctrinal errors (particularly as they affect the orthodox doctrine of Jesus Christ and His redemptive work), and to explore historically and practically the continued influence of semi-Pelagianism in the development of Christianity.

Semi-Pelagians shared the basic worldview of the Pelagians, in that they were opposed to Augustinian theology, particularly his predestination theory. They believed that an emphasis upon predestination stifled moral responsibility, producing in persons a sense of passivity towards life and fatalism for the future. Yet semi-Pelagians believed that Pelagius went too far in his attempt to counterbalance Augustinianism. Pelagius held that good works were the sole qualification for human salvation. The atoning blood of Jesus served only to give a fresh start for those who failed, but final acceptance from God came purely through human attainment of righteousness.

The semi-Pelagians disagreed with their mentor in their rejection of the notion of the moral perfectibility of natural humanity. They concurred with Scripture (and Augustine) that humans inevitably sin and stand in need of the grace of God. Yet in their desire to emphasize human responsibility in the salvation process, the semi-Pelagians erroneously introduced a synergistic dynamic to the Gospel formula that nullified the very nature of the grace that they espoused.

Definition

Historian Philip Schaff accurately defines the semi-Pelagian system of belief. "Its leading idea is, that divine grace and human will jointly accomplish the work of conversion and sanctification, and that ordinarily man must take the first step."[7] Admitting the role of God's grace in Christ, both in the dimensions of conversion and sanctification, the semi-Pelagians in effect contradict the nature of grace by requiring initial human conditions to be fulfilled before God's grace becomes available.

Scripture does not fail to emphasize human responsibility in the act of receiving the gift of salvation, but more than

---

[7] Philip Schaff, *History of the Christian Church, A.D. 311-600*, Vol. II, Edinburgh: T. and T. Clark, 1891, p. 858.

human responsibility is required to bring the sinner to a place of being able to benefit from the salvation that has been provided freely for all. God has taken the initiative through His grace and the Holy Spirit's intervention to prepare the sinner for conversion. Likewise, sanctification is not the result of the believer's initiative to take independent steps that merit the intervention of the Spirit's maturing presence. The initiative is God's, to draw the believer into deeper levels of sanctification.[8]

Initiative Belongs to God

The semi-Pelagians failed to see that the essence of human responsibility is in responding to the divine initiative, not in being the initiator. Initiative, which means 1) first step, origination; and 2) power or right to begin something, is the prerogative of the Giver, not the receiver. Even Jesus did not initiate the words and deeds that constituted His earthly life. As Son of Man, He submitted Himself to the human role of being a recipient of grace from the Father, even though He was the Giver of all life as Son of God. "I can do nothing on My own initiative," He stated in John 5:30. In John 8:28, Jesus said, "I do nothing on My own initiative, but I speak these things as the Father taught Me." The original sin was prompted by the adamic desire to step out of the responsive role as creature to become the

---

[8] The sanctifying presence of Christ is imputed to the believer at conversion. Yet conforming more completely to the character of Christ is a lifelong process. It is fair to say that sanctification is **a process of becoming who we already are in Christ.**

Initiator, the Creator. The semi-Pelagians failed to see that authentic human responsibility is to respond to the Creator's initiative, not to seize the initiative. The initiative belongs to God, both in conversion and in Christian maturity.

Chapter 4

Jesus as Gift: Semi-Pelagianism and Conversion

No Prevenient Grace

IN THIS CHAPTER, the conversion experience will be considered in isolation to highlight the conditionality injected by the semi-Pelagians into the Gospel of grace. Right from the beginning, we should notice that the semi-Pelagians wanted no part of the initial stage of the operation of God's grace as identified by Augustine, the stage known as prevenient grace. Prevenient grace is the theory that the grace of God resulting from Christ's redemptive work is actively drawing all humanity to a saving knowledge of Jesus Christ prior to any conscious awareness on the part of the recipient. Prevenient, or preventing, refers to the initiative of divine grace that prevents human control of the process until grace has completed its preparatory work to bring the sinner to a possible saving encounter with Christ. God's grace does not force conversion but overpowers the resistance of natural humanity until a decision is rendered either for or against Christ's saving love.

Sinners Have Capabilities
Disregarding the notion of prevenient grace, the semi-Pelagians viewed optimistically the capacity of natural humanity to take prerequisite, conditional steps that would move God to release His grace for actualizing the conversion experience. The semi-Pelagians admitted that grace alone actualizes conversion, but they believed that humans in the natural state can meet the conditions of repentance and faith that God required to release His saving grace. Thus, sinners were seen to be capable of achieving the conditions of repentance and faith without the aid of grace.

The Council's Ruling
The Council of Orange condemned such teaching. Several of the official articles of the Council recognized that preliminary actions by the sinner leading to the conversion experience are not performed apart from the process of God's grace. Prior to conscious awareness, the sinner has been the object of the Holy Spirit's loving, wooing and drawing influence, brought to the very precipice of the conversion experience by the purposive operation of God's grace. Canon 7 from the Council of Orange highlights the

position that the sinner can take no positive action in the direction of conversion without the Holy Spirit's influence.

> If anyone affirms that we can form any right opinion or make any right choice which relates to the salvation of eternal life, as is expedient for us, or that we can be saved, that is, assent to the preaching of the gospel through our natural powers without the illumination and inspiration of the Holy Spirit, who makes all men gladly assent to and believe in the truth, he is led astray by a heretical spirit, and does not understand the voice of God who says in the Gospel, "For apart from me you can do nothing" (John 15:5), and the word of the Apostle, "Not that we are competent of ourselves to claim anything as coming from us; our competence is from God" (2 Corinthians 3:5).

The biblical doctrine of conversion makes full allowance for the entrance of grace prior to conversion. The Holy Spirit, God's agent of conversion, visits the sinner with the gracious influence of the Gospel prior to the actual conversion experience. Recognizing that the natural capacity of sinful humanity is incapable of any level of self-help, the Holy Spirit comes to the aid of the sinner, enabling the sinner to respond appropriately to the initiative of the Gospel. Faith and repentance, components of conversion, are responses that can be made only through the Spirit's influence and enablement. God's gracious initiative must invade the life of the sinner, releasing the Spirit's presence and power, for conversion to be actualized.

Semi-Pelagianism fails to acknowledge, at this critical point in the conversion process, the Holy Spirit's role of positively influencing the sinner in the direction of the Gospel before the occurrence of new birth. The sinner is expected to improve his standing before God by his natural human efforts, thereby meriting the grace of God. Such naïve optimism inappropriately glorifies sinful humanity and compromises the sufficiency of God's grace in human conversion.

Joel's Prophecy
Joel prophetically envisioned the advent of the "last days" to be initiated by the momentous event of the Spirit's outpouring upon all humankind. Peter, preaching to the crowd of onlookers on the Day of Pentecost, did not hesitate to connect the "tongues of fire" manifested by the disciples that day with the fulfillment of Joel's ancient prophecy. He stated, "For these men are not drunk, as you suppose, for it is only the third hour of the day; but this is what was spoken of through the prophet Joel: 'And it shall be in the last days,' God said, 'that I will pour out My Spirit upon all mankind;'" (Acts 2:15-17 NAS) Peter recognized that the Spirit's power being poured out upon the church was but a fraction of the universal measure of the Spirit's outpouring then descending upon the earth's

inhabitants. Human history has never been the same since that day.

Grace Prior to Conversion

The significance of the Day of Pentecost events cannot be overestimated. We find the resurrected, triumphant Jesus now ascended to heaven fulfilling His promise to baptize His church with the Holy Spirit, while simultaneously pouring out the Spirit upon all living flesh. A common purpose links these dual outpourings. While Jesus was empowering His church to "go into all the world and preach the gospel to all creation," (Mark 16:15) He was also facilitating the evangelistic mission by releasing the Holy Spirit upon all human flesh.

Thus, from the Day of Pentecost onwards, the Holy Spirit has been released both to empower the church and to encounter every human creature. The Scriptures do not make it clear just how the earth's inhabitants are impacted by the Spirit's visitation. However, the New Testament is definite about the Holy Spirit's vital connection with the risen Jesus and His Gospel message. A primary mission of the Holy Spirit is to glorify Jesus (John 16:14) and to bear witness of Him (John 15:26). God's grace was demonstrated in the accomplishment of redemption through the finished work of Jesus, and God's grace continues to be manifest through the Holy Spirit's outpouring upon the peoples of the earth, glorifying Jesus and testifying of Him.

New Testament Conversion

Peter's interpretation of Joel's prophecy provides the New Testament rationale for the church's evangelistic enterprise. The doctrine of conversion cannot be rightly formulated without factoring in the "Pentecostal" perspective. Peter's sermon leads us to conclude that no one is converted to Jesus independent of the saving influence of God and His grace. Jesus' death for the sins of the world was not an isolated event but was a pivotal point in world history. As Jesus stated in John's Gospel, "'And I, if I be lifted up from the earth, will draw all men to Myself.' But He was saying this to indicate the kind of death by which He was to die." (John 12:32-33) The Holy Spirit has been poured out upon all of humanity, and the message of Jesus' cross conveyed by the Spirit carries with it the power of salvation. (I Corinthians 1:18)

Sinners Are Drawn to Christ

God the Father also works through the Spirit's influence to draw lost humanity to His Son and His redemption. John's Gospel relates Jesus' words, "No one can come to Me, unless the Father who sent Me draws him; and I will raise him up on the last day." (John 6:44) Everyone who is privileged to share in Jesus' resurrection in the last day has been drawn to Him by Father God. Semi-Pelagians fail to understand the means whereby persons are converted to Jesus. No one makes oneself a candidate for conversion by their own actions independent of the grace of God. Each member of the Triune God (Father, Son and Holy Spirit) participates in the work of preparing sinners to receive the Gospel of grace.

Such a scenario suggests questions of utmost seriousness concerning the nature of the Semi-Pelagian "gospel." Does God dispense the grace of His salvation according to the performance of certain merits demonstrated by lost humanity? Is God's grace conditioned upon the satisfactory completion of prerequisites, preparing potential converts to be worthy of salvation? Semi-Pelagianism answers "Yes" to these questions. The church, however, must counter with a resounding "No" to both, unless we are prepared to sacrifice God's grace on the altar of human performance.

Semi-Pelagianism Adds Works to Grace
Semi-Pelagianism reduces salvation to a system of works plus grace. Yet the church's proclamation of the Gospel maintains its integrity precisely because it is a Gospel of grace, irrespective of any human prerequisites, merits or works. Jesus states clearly that "apart from Me you can do nothing." (John 15:5) Jesus and His grace are not held at bay until we present evidence that we deserve His visitation. Paul remarks that we were both "helpless" and "ungodly" when Jesus took decisive action to die for us (Romans 5:6). How dare we presume that we must perform satisfactorily as sinners before God's grace is made available to us. Semi-Pelagianism clings to a

standard of human performance precluding the entrance of grace, thus it represents a rejection of the very essence of the Christian Gospel.

Chapter 5

Jesus as Gift: Semi-Pelagianism and Sanctification

Semi-Pelagian View of Sanctification

RECALLING PHILIP SCHAFF'S astute observations from Chapter 3, semi-Pelagianism not only denies the exclusiveness of divine grace in the conversion experience, but also introduces a synergism of grace and the human will in sanctification. And in each dimension of Christian experience, humanity must take the first step. Our purposes in this chapter are to explore why such errors regarding sanctification are fatal to the Gospel, and to counter with considerations of Christian maturity more faithful to the Biblical witness.

I want to clarify the meaning of sanctification as I see it before proceeding further. Sanctification is commonly understood in Christian circles as a process whereby the believer grows in deeper conformity to the character and teachings of Christ. This is a part of the maturation of the

Christian as old habits change, the mind is renewed, and transformation progresses through the work of the Holy Spirit. But there is no question that there is indisputable Biblical support also for the position that the sanctification of the believer also occurs instantaneously at conversion. Sanctification is to become holy and righteous as Jesus is, and when the new birth occurs, Jesus comes to dwell inside the believer through the Holy Spirit. The new believer is "one spirit with Him (Christ)." (I Corinthians 6:17) When we are in Christ, we have imputed to us everything that He is. Since Jesus is sanctified (John 17:19) we are sanctified with His sanctification. On the other hand, there is plentiful Biblical support that sanctification includes a process of growth, discipline and renewal that brings us ever closer in conformity to the character and teachings of Jesus. The best way that I can describe the totality of sanctification is this. **We are in a process of becoming what we already are in Christ.** We are sanctified, yet we are continually being sanctified through the Holy Spirit. The Wuest translation of Revelation 22:11 beautifully captures this dynamic. "And he who is holy (sanctified), let him be made holy (sanctified) still."

It may seem to some that this discussion is a diversion from the issues of our study. Yet that is not the case. A key reason why many Christians fall into the semi-Pelagian performance trap after conversion is because they do not know that they are sanctified. The Christian life becomes for them a rigorous and demanding agenda of striving and working to be like Jesus. Although Christian maturity is a process of growth, it is not an attempt to attain acceptance with God or gain right standing with Him. Every Christian needs to know at the very beginning that they are considered by the Father to be holy and righteous in Christ. No amount of works and good deeds can add or take away from that. Armed with that glorious truth, they are set free by God's grace to bear fruit for the Kingdom. Grace and gratitude replaces ceaseless striving after the very thing they have already attained.

Jesus Not in Control

Turning now to the progressive aspect of sanctification as viewed by the semi-Pelagians, they falsely assume that Christians control this process. They think that the sanctifying presence of the Holy Spirit only operates when believers initiate actions to invoke the Spirit's intervention. They think that God's grace is apportioned according to successful human performance. This erroneous belief injects into the equation an unwarranted weight of burden for the Christian not set forth in Scripture.

Although semi-Pelagians view Jesus as the supreme Lord of history, yet they see Him as having voluntarily restricted the activity of His Holy Spirit until the church takes the appropriate steps to "trigger" His intervention. So, who is really Lord of history, if Jesus and the activity of His Spirit are under the control of human initiative? The semi-Pelagian scheme requires that human works precede and regulate the operation of God's grace in Christ.

Faith a Performance
For instance, semi-Pelagians are guilty of abusing the Biblical doctrine of faith. They view faith as a capacity within the believer capable of being expressed without the enablement of Christ and the Spirit. The believer must first express the appropriate measure of faith before Jesus allows the Spirit to intervene. God's grace and corresponding benefits are conditionally rewarded only as the believer exhibits proper faith. In each display of the believer's faith, God evaluates the level of performance as a basis for determining the nature of His involvement and the measure of benefits to be imparted. Since every performance must measure up, believers are pressured to seek various techniques expected to elevate their faith.

Not only faith, but other types of legitimate Christian activity such as prayer, fasting, giving and other forms of service suffer similar abuse when transformed into tools of self-interest. When these activities are misapplied to become spiritual techniques meant to solicit special privileges and benefits from God, then they have lost their connection with the Gospel of Jesus Christ.

Minimizes the Bible's Worth
This reduction of the Gospel to a performance agenda often causes believers to minimize the true worth of the

Bible, making it a repository of benefits promised by God to His people if certain behavioral conditions are satisfied. Faith becomes the behavioral norm that, when performed successfully, releases the benefits of God. This perspective conditions God's activity based upon the accomplishments of His people both to acquire knowledge of His benefits as specified in the Bible and to demonstrate the appropriate measure of faith warranting His intervention.

Augustine and Faith

Historically, the issue of faith was a pivotal factor in the resolution both of the Pelagian and semi-Pelagian controversies. What made the difference was Augustine's dramatic reversal of opinion, leading him to reject the notion that Biblical faith is a human work. He concluded after much deliberation that faith should not be considered an independent human work, but rather a gift from God. This conclusion later proved to be a hedge of doctrinal defense against the subtlety of Pelagian and semi-Pelagian errors. A verse from the Pauline book of *I Corinthians* sealed Augustine's position on this issue. "And what do you have that you did not receive? But if you did receive it, why do you boast as if you had not received it?" (I Corinthians 4:7) As Augustine came to see, even the faith to believe in the Gospel of Jesus and to live dependently upon Him is not to be considered a work of merit, but a gift of God's grace.

Authentic Faith

When faith is viewed rightly as a product of God's grace, then the authentic Gospel is preserved. This truthful presupposition necessarily excludes the view that faith is a product of the believer, independent of divine enablement. Faith should not be viewed as a qualifying work on the part of believers meant to control God's gracious intervention. God is gracious in His innermost being and the impartation of His grace does not depend upon the performance of His children. The gift to humanity of Jesus Christ and His salvation demonstrates fully that God is gracious on the highest level. God is gracious, and desires that His children respond positively to His initiatives. Yet He is not depleted of grace when His children fail to reciprocate. The grace of God is bigger than the believer's lapses into sin and the Holy Spirit uses both failures and successes in a delicate process of weaving all the experiences of every Christian into a beautiful tapestry of Christian maturity (Romans 8:28).

God Controls the Process of Christian Maturity
The maturation of the believer is a lifelong process under God's control and must not be reduced to a succession of performance initiatives exercised by believers, as semi-Pelagians contend. Believers are "new creatures" in Christ (II Corinthians 5:17) and are no longer dominated by fleshly behavior but live by the Spirit of God (Romans 8:9). Yet fleshly behavior remains a possibility when Christ's cross and Lordship are not applied continuously in Christian living.

The Sin of Presumption

A disastrous aspect of semi-Pelagianism is its tendency to sanction fleshly behavior over against Spirit-led behavior by advocating that initiative is the prerogative of the believer. The Bible identifies this type of error as the sin of presumption. King David prayed that he be guarded from presumptuous sins (Psalms 19:13). One of the four temptations Jesus resisted in the wilderness was the sin of presumption. Satan took Jesus to the pinnacle of the temple, and challenged Him to jump off, citing God's promises of angelic protection. Jesus detected the flaw in Satan's use of Scriptural promises. He countered by quoting a different Scripture: "You shall not tempt the Lord your God." Jesus' words may also be rendered, "You shall not put the Lord your God to the test." The essence of this temptation was to challenge Jesus to initiate a course of action not directed by God, yet to utilize a Scriptural promise to force God to intervene. God is not a pawn to be controlled by the whims of His people. God honors submission to His initiative but does not respond to presumptuous efforts to manipulate His will.

Presumption from the Old Testament

An Old Testament example of the sin of presumption is represented by the children of Israel under Moses' leadership, as they experienced their first opportunity to take the Promised Land. The twelve spies, except for Joshua and Caleb, brought back a negative report relating to the difficulty of occupying the land of Canaan. The negative report had the effect of discouraging the children of Israel from obeying God and responding to His promise of victory and conquest. Instead, they refused to follow God's command to take the land. In view of the disobedience of God's children, God withdrew His promise of victory and sent His people back into the wilderness to wander for another forty years.

When faced with the sentence of more wilderness wandering, a faction of the people changed their mind and decided to march into battle to take the land. This presumptuous move was their own plan, for God had withdrawn His promise of successful conquest. God refused to back them, and they went into battle on their own strength. The result predictably was disastrous. Moses summarized the outcome. "So I spoke to you, but you would not listen. Instead you rebelled against the command of the Lord, and acted presumptuously and went up into the hill country. And the Amorites who live in that hill country came out against you, and chased you as bees do, and crushed you from Seir to Hormah." (Deuteronomy 1:43-44)

Presumptuous Living
Semi-Pelagianism condones presumption as the proper course of action for Christians. Rather than living as responders to the Spirit's initiative, believers are challenged to act on their own initiative, presuming that

God will get involved because of their performance. Semi-Pelagians advocate that Christians live every day with such a sequence of behavior. God begins as a spectator, waiting for the believer to initiate a course of action presumed to be a precondition meriting His intervention. If the action is successfully performed, God graciously comes on the scene and manifests His benefits. As this sequence is repeated over the course of a lifetime, the believer grows in sanctification because of God's system of rewards for good behavior.

Presumption is Heresy

The Council of Orange in 529 rejected this semi-Pelagian view of sanctification. Canon 6 addresses the false assumption that the intervention of God and His grace is a reward of Christian performance.

> "If anyone says that God has mercy upon us when, apart from his grace, we believe, will, desire, strive, labor, pray, watch, study, seek, ask, or knock, but does not confess that it is by the infusion and inspiration of the Holy Spirit within us that we have the faith, the will, or the strength to do all these things as we ought; or if anyone makes the assistance of grace depend on the humility or obedience of man and does not agree that it is a gift of grace itself that we are obedient and humble, he contradicts the Apostle who says, 'What have you that you did not receive?' (I

Corinthians 4:7), and, 'But by the grace of God I am what I am.' (I Corinthians 15:10)"

The bishops at Orange also noted from Jesus' teachings that the life required to produce fruit does not come from the branch, but from the Vine. Fruit is not the reward for the branch's performance but is the result of an abiding relationship with the Vine. Canon 23 refutes the Performance/Spectator motif of semi-Pelagianism.

> "Concerning the branches of the vine. The branches on the vine do not give life to the vine, but receive life from it; thus the vine is related to its branches in such a way that it supplies them with what they need to live, and does not take this from them. Thus it is to the advantage of the disciples, not Christ, both to have Christ abiding in them and to abide in Christ. For if the vine is cut down another can shoot up from the live root; but one who is cut off from the vine cannot live without the root (John 15:5ff)."

In Scripture, no separation or distance between the believer and the Holy Spirit is indicated, nor is the believer expected to perform "for God." Jesus desires willing and loving submission from His people. Intimate relationship is the means that He guides His children into the further reaches of His purpose. How preposterous and arrogant is the notion that we manipulate Jesus to grant our wishes by using His Word as a legal contract to force His hand to act. Jesus has His own timing and way to orchestrate history, and our total submission to His Lordship better prepares us to know and yield to the direction of His Spirit.

Chapter 6

Jesus as Gift: Semi-Pelagianism to the Present Day

Semi-Pelagianism Permitted

ALTHOUGH CONDEMNED AS HERESY by the Council of Orange in 529, semi-Pelagian doctrine managed to resurface at various times throughout the church's history in varied disguises to challenge the essential truth of the unconditional nature of God's grace in Jesus Christ. Ancient semi-Pelagianism was not able to generate universal support yet advocates of this doctrine in some cases not only avoided the censorship of heresy but managed to maintain general respect within Christendom. This represents an enigma that seems to characterize semi-Pelagianism. Despite the undisputed sentence of heresy levied against the ancient expression, new forms of this doctrine have navigated beneath the church's radar screen without detection, jettisoning its destructive cargo among the faithful.

When semi-Pelagian presuppositions capture the thinking of a generation of Christians, a "Pharasaic" style of Christianity enshrouds the church. Human traditions begin to infiltrate Christian beliefs and practices, submerging believers in a sea of performance activities not initiated by the Spirit of God.

Numerous expressions of semi-Pelagianism have surfaced within Christendom after the Council of Orange. By failing to take a stand against this heresy, the church's toleration has had the effect of sanctioning its presence. All three major branches of Christendom, whether Catholic, Protestant or Eastern Orthodox, have allowed semi-Pelagian beliefs to coexist peacefully with established orthodoxy. As a result, Gospel truths have been weakened and, in some cases, corrupted because of compromise.

Flesh Allowed to Dominate the Spirit

The gravest danger of semi-Pelagianism is its subtle attack upon the truth that God's grace through the gift of Jesus Christ is the only basis for knowing God. In times when the church tolerates the presence of this heresy, human actions can rival the work of God's grace both in conversion and sanctification, with human initiative controlling the process. When semi-Pelagian tendencies dominate, fleshly activities masquerade in Christian disguise while the legitimate operations of the Holy Spirit suffer decline.

Catholic Toleration

Late Medieval Catholicism is a prime example of a church easily misled by semi-Pelagian presuppositions. As the dominance of Scholasticism subsided after Thomas Aquinas, tendencies towards semi-Pelagianism increased. Even Thomas, in unguarded moments, seemed to invite misinterpretation. A case in point is the following discussion: "...man of himself, and without the external help of grace, can prepare himself for grace. Further, man prepares himself for grace by doing what is in him to do, since, if man does what is in him to do, God will not deny him grace."[9] In other instances, Aquinas legitimated the need for human merits, both prior to conversion and in the sanctification process. After Aquinas, the theologies of William of Ockham and Gabriel Biel further fortified the presence of semi-Pelagianism in late Medieval theology.

Luther's Alternative

Martin Luther's troubled conscience reacted adversely to the established dogma of sixteenth century Catholicism precisely because the church under semi-Pelagian influence applauded human merit unaided by divine grace. Luther instinctively knew that even his best efforts were corrupted by sin. As he pored over the Scriptures in preparation for his university teaching assignments, his explorations led to the discovery of the essential content of

---

[9] Thomas Aquinas, *The Summa Theologica*, II-I, q. 109, art. 6, obj. 1 and 2. Ed. Anton C. Pegis, *Basic Writings of Saint Thomas Aquinas*, Vol. II, New York: Random House, 1945, p. 987.

the doctrine of justification. Put simply, our relationship with God is purely the product of divine grace through the gift of Jesus Christ.

As a Catholic priest, monk and professor, Luther's developing theological insights had the potential of bringing renewal to a church that had lost touch with the Gospel. Yet an unforeseen set of circumstances thrust Luther into unavoidable conflict with the Catholic establishment, closing the door on any real possibility of mutual communication.

Opportunity Lost

Luther's 1517 academic critique, the Ninety-five Theses, directed at abuses he detected in Pope Leo X's Jubilee Indulgence, unexpectedly seized the attention of the entire Holy Roman Empire. Luther's bold criticisms captured the imagination of a populace already intensely disenchanted with the Roman church and her internal corruptions and lack of spiritual power. Luther probably had no knowledge when he posted his theses that the Pope and a leading Archbishop of the church had major financial investments that were dependent upon the success of the Jubilee Indulgence. As public attention turned to Luther's criticisms, the success of the campaign suddenly became jeopardized. The church viewed Luther as an expendable commodity to be silenced before irreparable damage was done. Luther only wanted a hearing to defend his views. Instead, after refusing to recant his position, he found himself excommunicated from the only Christian church in the Empire.

Prior to his excommunication, Luther had devoted his efforts to helping his church rediscover the doctrine of justification, rejecting performance-based approaches in favor of grace only through the gift of Jesus Christ. Having been cast out of that church, Luther was forced to redirect his focus upon the formidable task of formulating a new ecclesiological structure for himself and others who had been alienated from Catholicism.

Protestant Beginnings

As Luther was thrust in the role of starting a new Christian movement, he maintained remarkable consistency in grounding all doctrines and practices in the foundational truth that justification is a product of God's grace alone, and no human works other than those accomplished by Jesus Christ contribute in any way to the reconciliation freely extended to the human race. In the Lutheran model, even the good works of Christians are not to be viewed as initiatives from the human side intended to merit God's grace and favor, but rather are to be Spirit influenced responses to the grace and favor of God already bestowed through Jesus Christ. Now having the luxury of looking back upon the development of Protestantism, we would be hard pressed to find any period of theological history freer of semi-Pelagian influence than in the early days of Luther's leadership of the Protestant movement.

Council of Trent: Bastion of Semi-Pelagianism

The Catholic Church had not been predisposed to pay heed to Luther's views while he served as a Catholic priest, so it hardly needs to be said that they were unwilling to give him a hearing now that he had become the dominant voice of a rival ecclesiastical body outside their official boundaries. As the Counter Reformation of the Catholic Church took shape at the Council of Trent (1545-1563), acquiescence to Protestant doctrinal challenges was not a consideration. The Catholic bishops were bent on ratifying a status quo doctrinal and practical agenda heavily laden with semi-Pelagian assumptions.

Most revealing was Trent's explication of the doctrine of justification. Catholic theology codified its synergistic orientation by asserting that works of love must accompany the gift of God's grace for justification to be validated. Faith alone in the redemptive triumph of Jesus Christ is not enough. Furthermore, the cooperative venture between human works of charity plus God's grace must result in an acquired, inherent righteousness in the believer, necessitating that justification be viewed as a lifelong process. Eternity with God is not assured until the final judgment, when the righteous works of the believer must meet the ultimate test of the holiness of God.

Trent represents a model case study of the semi-Pelagian error. Any formula for justification that attempts to add performance-oriented merits to the grace of God as a basis for God's ultimate acceptance logically contradicts the very essence of God's grace. The apostle Paul clarifies the only valid doctrine of justification. Grace must stand alone. "But if it is by grace, it is no longer on the basis of works, otherwise grace is no longer grace." (Romans 11:6) And assurance must be of the very essence of faith, for justification is a gift based upon the past accomplishments of Jesus Christ, completed on the cross of Calvary. Human works can neither add nor take away from the finished work of Jesus Christ on the cross. Justification is based solely upon the victory that was finished on the cross, and it is actualized in the individual simply by believing in the accomplishment of Jesus.

Protestantism After Luther

Catholic theology remained oblivious to her semi-Pelagian bedfellow long after Trent's permissive sanction of a works-based doctrine of justification. Luther detected the Catholic problem but found no acceptance from the mother church to make a positive difference. An outcast, he charted a new course on the secure foundation of Pauline theology, enhanced by Augustinianism. Yet after Luther's promising beginnings, later generations of Protestants departed from his founding vision. Semi-Pelagian views infiltrated various Protestant groups, compromising the doctrinally sound beginnings of the movement.

Protestantism has progressed into the modern era naively harboring the subtly of semi-Pelagian influence. Few periods have escaped the corruption of this pestilent heresy. The presence of semi-Pelagianism can be detected in Calvinism after Calvin, in Lutheran Pietism, in the Wesleyan movement and Methodism, in the American Awakenings, in European Liberalism, and in American Evangelicalism. The Pentecostal and Charismatic movements of the twentieth century are no exception.

Evangelical Error

American Evangelicalism, riding upon revivalist practices characteristic of colonial and early American Awakening movements, views conversion in a semi-Pelagian fashion. Evangelicals generally recognize conversion as a work of divine grace, made available to humanity exclusively through the redemptive work of Jesus Christ. Yet the grace that actualizes conversion is portrayed as being locked up and inaccessible until prerequisite actions on the part of the sinner are performed. The sinner must perform acts of repentance and faith, without divine assistance, to qualify for the activation of grace and the Holy Spirit's converting work.

Evangelistic appeals aimed at converting sinners challenge individuals to repent, that is, to turn away from their sinful practices, and to make a personal commitment to Jesus Christ. Some preachers attempt to move the emotions, some appeal to the intellect, while others try to move the will of the hearer. In any case, the common assumption is that sinners must take the first step, satisfying God's conditions of repentance and faith, before He takes reciprocal action by imparting His grace to actualize the conversion experience. Furthermore, such a mindset assumes that sinners are capable of repenting and having faith in their natural, sinful state, apart from the presence and influence of God's grace.

The Spirit's Influence
Evangelicals who embrace these beliefs probably are unaware that they are operating from a semi-Pelagian rather than a Scriptural model. The Scriptures reveal that God is graciously working in the lives of sinners prior to any conscious acknowledgment of such actions. Peter indicated that the Holy Spirit had been poured out upon "all flesh" on the Day of Pentecost, soon after Jesus' ascension to heaven. (Acts 2:16-17) Speaking of His crucifixion for the sins of the whole world, Jesus said, "And I, if I be lifted up from the earth, will draw all men to Myself." (John 12:32) God the Father graciously orchestrates this drawing influence administered through Christ and by the Holy Spirit. Jesus stated, "No one can come to Me, unless the Father who sent Me draws him; and I will raise him up on the last day." (John 6:44) Those who come to Christ in the new birth are revealing that their actions are not totally their own but have been "wrought in God" from the beginning. (John 3:21)

Faith and Repentance

Another common Evangelical error related to conversion deserves treatment here, for its roots are semi-Pelagian. This view holds that repentance precedes conversion. The logic follows that sinners must reject their sinful practices so that they will be presentable to Christ. Once sin is abandoned, faith in Jesus becomes the final step from the human side. He rewards those who have satisfactorily performed the preparatory action He deems worthy of redemption and releases His grace to finalize the process.

Reformer John Calvin insightfully dismissed such non-Scriptural thinking in his *Institutes of the Christian Religion*. States Calvin, "There are some, however, who suppose that repentance precedes faith, rather than flows from it, or is produced by it as fruit from a tree." "Now it ought to be a fact beyond controversy that repentance not only constantly follows faith, but is also born of faith."[10] (III.3.1) The instant that the sinner receives Jesus as Redeemer, the gift of faith is produced, actualizing the new birth of the sinner. The Holy Spirit now inhabits the new believer, empowering the recipient to take steps of genuine repentance. In the light of Christ's presence, the believer can distinguish the darkness of sin and turn away from it. Without faith already being present through a living encounter with Christ, true repentance is impossible. The

---

[10] *Institutes of the Christian Religion*, ed. John T. McNeill, trans. Ford Lewis Battles, Volume I, Philadelphia: The Westminster Press, 1960, p. 593 (III.3.1).

sinner, unaided by divine grace, does not have the discerning ability or the power to turn away from sinful practices.

The Performance Trap
Semi-Pelagian errors related to the sanctification process are evidenced in many groups. These Christians fall into the trap of performance-oriented living. They think that because they lived for the devil prior to being born again, now they must compensate by living for Jesus Christ, as if He is now a spectator in heaven evaluating Christian behavior. Performance that pleases Him, He rewards with His divine sanction and blessing. Sub-par performance, He disciplines. Believers desiring superior blessings and manifestations think that they must demonstrate higher levels of faith. They take upon themselves the challenge of initiating spiritual practices sure to qualify them for uncommon supernatural impartations.

This orientation becomes a trap, because prayer, fasting, Bible reading and meditation, speaking in tongues, praise and worship, etc., are legitimate activities never meant to be used as merits offered to God to solicit His manifest presence and supernatural privileges. Such favors are not to be purchased by works but are to be appropriated as gifts of Christ's presence already indwelling every believer.

Legalism in Galatia

Performance oriented Christianity at its root is a fleshly version of the Gospel like the problematic perspective plaguing the Galatian church in the days of the apostle Paul. Chastising the Galatians for their legalistic mentality, Paul asserts, "Are you so foolish? Having begun by the Spirit, are you now being perfected by the flesh?" (Galatians 3:3) The Galatians had begun well, gaining their freedom by simple faith in response to Paul's proclamation of the Gospel of grace. But certain Judaizers were threatening to rob them of their freedom by attempting to force them to obey the Mosaic Law as a condition to maintain God's presence and blessings. Paul declared to the Galatian church, "It was for freedom that Christ set us free; therefore keep standing firm and do not be subject again to a yoke of slavery." (Galatians 5:1) Paul explained that Christians are called to abide in Christ and walk in faith by the Holy Spirit. To depend on external standards of performance, whether the Law of Moses or any formula of good works, when employed as a conditional step to acquire God's presence and benefits, is a falling away from God's grace into a fleshly scheme of working for God.

Led by the Spirit

The Gospel counters the semi-Pelagian performance orientation by affirming two critical truths. 1) Faith is not a performance, but a continuous submission to the initiative of the Holy Spirit, directing our lives according to the Lordship of Jesus Christ. 2) Christians do not live **for** Jesus, but rather, have died to self-life and have become **vessels**

of the indwelling Christ through the Spirit's presence. Earlier in his letter, Paul brought together all the essential elements of living in the freedom of the Gospel of grace. "I have been crucified with Christ; and it is no longer I who live, but Christ lives in me; and the life which I now live in the flesh I live by faith in the Son of God, who loved me, and delivered Himself up for me." (Galatians 2:20) Jesus' presence, blessings and power are not external goals to be acquired by superior spiritual performance but are freely bestowed giftings that accompany Christ's presence. The Spirit does not respond to the believer's works but leads the believer to respond to the works of Christ in His continuing mission in the earth.

The Tendency to Resist God's Grace
Modern Christians continue to fall prey to the trap that has ensnared multitudes of believers since the days of Paul. We have trouble really believing that our Gospel is a Gospel of grace. Rather than gratefully receiving Jesus Christ and the full endowment of giftings and benefits associated with His baptism in the Spirit, we are tempted to fall back into carnality by attempting to do something for God to reciprocate for our good fortune. We want to demonstrate to God, to others, and to ourselves, that He made the right choice when He selected us. We are repelled at the thought of being objects of charity, chosen purely out of His desire to show mercy rather than because of something within us that merited His favor.

Trying to Compete with God

Yet when we fail to accept our status of freedom in Christ solely based on His gracious will, we quickly nullify our freedom by becoming slaves again to fleshly self-centeredness. By trying to add our accomplishments to the incomparable story of God's redemptive triumph in Christ, we only succeed in detracting from His success and revealing that we don't really comprehend that our position in Christ was sealed for us while we were absolutely helpless. When Christians are found to be trying to impress God, to measure up, to do something for God, or to obtain the blessings of the abundant life by spiritual performances, they are displaying symptoms of immature, fleshly behavior. Paul demolishes the performance orientation of semi-Pelagianism: "For I will not presume to speak of anything except what Christ has accomplished through me, …" (Romans 15:18)

Total Glory to the Lord

Those liberated by the Gospel give no place for self glory. They recognize the handiwork of God in all good things, and delight in giving Him exclusive and total glory. The Psalmist understood the basic truth. "For I will not trust in my bow, nor will my sword save me. …In God we have boasted all day long. And we will give thanks to Thy name forever." (Psalms 44:6, 8) Again, we turn to Paul for definitive revelation of the need for the believer to give due recognition for every part of the abundant and eternal life imparted through God's grace in Christ Jesus. "But by

His doing you are in Christ Jesus, who became to us wisdom from God, and righteousness and sanctification and redemption, that, just as it is written, 'Let Him who boasts, boast in the Lord." (I Corinthians 1:30-31)

Chapter 7

Jesus as Example: Spirit Dependency

PROCEEDING TO THE SECOND PART of Luther's statement, "Christ is first gift, then example," we direct our attention to the truth that Jesus is our example. Some readers may doubt that a biblical basis exists for such an affirmation. From the apostle Peter, we find solid evidence. "For you have been called for this purpose, since Christ also suffered for you, leaving you an example for you to follow in His steps, …" (I Peter 2:21) The apostle John offers additional reinforcement. "…the one who says he abides in Him ought himself to walk in the same manner as He walked." (I John 2:6) John continues, "…as He is, so also are we in this world." (I John 4:17) But Jesus is not a dead hero, whose teachings and lifestyle are to be followed as a model for contemporary inspiration and emulation. Because of His resurrection and impartation of the Holy Spirit, Jesus is the only dead hero who has come back to life to indwell and direct the lives of His people.

Exercise in Futility

After exposing the fallacy of semi-Pelagianism in previous chapters, it should be beyond question that persons relying solely upon their own natural resources, without the presence and enablement of the Holy Spirit, have no possibility of following Jesus' example. Even to attempt such an endeavor is an exercise in futility. Had Jesus Himself attempted to live the life set before Him without the indwelling of the Spirit provided by His Father, He would have failed miserably. In His humanity, Jesus was never without the fullness of the Holy Spirit (John 3:34-35). The Holy Spirit was the source of His ability to speak the words and do the works of His heavenly Father. His absolute yieldedness and total dependency upon the Holy Spirit enabled Jesus to fulfill completely His personal mission and destiny.

The Law: Built-in Failure

A parallel illustration can be found in the dilemma faced by the Jews as they were presented with the obligation to live by the standard of conduct specified by the Mosaic Law. God's commandments regulated every area of human life, and no one was able to comply perfectly with its statutes. The Law aroused mixed reactions for the Jew. Although God's glory was revealed through the Law, yet the Law also magnified human sin (Romans 3:20). The Law was given for a dual purpose. It was given to reveal something of God's character and of His behavioral obligations to be followed in covenant relationship among His people. Yet beyond its purpose as a code of conduct, the Law was given to reveal the finitude, futility and failure of fallen humanity to please God apart from His provision of a Messiah. Failure was built into the Jewish system of worship, in that animal sacrifices were necessary as a sacrificial atonement for human sin. Such atoning sacrifices foreshadowed the coming of the Messiah, whose own blood was shed as a permanent sacrifice and atonement for the people's sins. The Mosaic Law brought human sin to light, and confronted Jews with the realization that their only hope of attaining the righteousness of God would be through their dependency upon the gift of Messiah, God's own Son.

Death to the Natural Way
When Jesus the Messiah died on the cross of Calvary, all attempts by natural humanity to attain personal righteousness and gain the favor of God met their death. After Calvary, the only acceptable way to experience relationship with God is to abandon all efforts of personal initiative and surrender to God's gracious initiative. God has provided no other way of entering into relationship with Himself than to accept freely the gift of His only Son Jesus. The moment that Jesus is received, the Holy Spirit comes to dwell in the life of the believer. Of all who receive Him, Jesus stakes His claim as Lord of that life, and begins the process of exercising His initiative to gain and maintain full control. The personal mission and destiny of the life of the individual believer can be achieved only as

the Holy Spirit is given freedom to enforce the Lordship of Jesus in every facet of thought and action.

Failure of the Liberal Ideal

Particularly in the context of Liberal Protestantism in 19th century Europe, the biblical revelation of Jesus was replaced by an image of Jesus as a romantic idealist who modeled love for God and concern for His fellow humans. Jesus was portrayed as a cross-cultural embodiment of universal love for all people, and a general model of how everyone should love God and others. Sin was simply the absence of loving concern, which could be remedied by modeling the love that Jesus exemplified. Such lofty idealism certainly inspired a temporary sense of good will and altruism, but ultimately left in its wake the decidedly bitter taste of discouragement and defeat. Ideals unsupported by the solid foundation of Truth crash and crumble in the face of the frontal attacks of sin. Jesus' lifestyle of consistent love stands as a definitive indictment against fanciful humanistic prescriptions oozing with positive intentions and pious resolutions. Sin must be crucified by the cross of Jesus, and life regenerated by the invasion of the Holy Spirit.

Jesus: Temporary Amnesia

Part of the humiliation of the Incarnation for the Son of God was His voluntary, although temporary, surrender of the privileges and prerogatives of His Godhead position. For our sakes and for our salvation He willingly limited

Himself to the conditions of incarnate humanity. The apostle Paul captures the depth of condescension willingly endured by the Son of God. "...although He existed in the form of God, did not regard equality with God a thing to be grasped, but emptied Himself, taking the form of a bondservant, and being made in the likeness of men." (Philippians 2:6-7) Memory of His previous life within the Godhead was temporarily unavailable to Him. This could legitimately be called a state of temporary amnesia. When He assumed His new identity as Son of Man, He did not continue to be engaged in the consciousness and experience of His divine nature. Certainly, He maintained His divine identity. A big part of His redemptive mission was to communicate to a skeptical world that He was God's Son. But His divine nature and experience was not available to Him as He took on His human identity as Jesus of Nazareth.

Jesus: Natural Human Development

As Jesus of Nazareth, He fully entered life as a human, developing naturally within the conditions of finitude. As Luke reveals, "And the Child continued to grow and become strong, increasing in wisdom; and the grace of God was upon Him. ...And Jesus kept increasing in wisdom and stature, and in favor with God and men." (Luke 2:40, 52) Although His inherent nature was divine, He voluntarily restricted His access to the resources of His divinity to be true to the realm of His humanity. Consciously, He knew that He was Son of God, but He had no memory of His life and experience as a member of the Godhead. His only conscious memories were His life as Mary's son. He knew that He had an identity beyond His human life and experience, but He gave up His natural access to His divine identity from conception to the grave.

While developing within His human identity, Jesus was "dead" to His divine nature. Jesus spoke often of the "cross" before He literally experienced death on the Cross of Calvary. His cross before Calvary, in part, was the crucifixion that He was living out in connection with His divine position. Jesus was very God, and He knew that, but the privileges and prerogatives associated with His divine life were not available to Him as Son of Man. At times, Jesus must have longed to have been able to step out of His humanity and awaken to His experience as God's eternal Son. Yet the mission that He must accomplish, as Messiah and Savior, necessitated that He submit fully to Adam's position and nature. As the Second Adam, His obedience to the Father's will needed to be authentically human. Reliance upon His divine nature would have contradicted the authenticity of His human nature and experience.

The Source of Jesus' Divine Life
Yet Jesus' human life, from conception onwards, was never governed solely by natural human capacities. The presence of divinity was always with Him. Yet that presence of divinity that He depended upon was not His

nature as Son of God. Having yielded to His Father's will to undergo the Incarnation, He relinquished any right to draw upon the resources of His divine nature. But another dimension of divine presence was made available by the Father for the Son of Man. As the apostle John asserts, "...for God giveth not the Spirit by measure unto Him. The Father loveth the Son, and hath given all things into his hand." (John 3:34-35, KJV) The Holy Spirit indwelt and filled Jesus' human life, so that divine, supernatural presence and capacity was always with Him. That the presence of divinity within Jesus' humanity was the Holy Spirit, and not His own divine nature as God's Son, is a matter of immense doctrinal significance.

Real Humanity, Real Obedience

At this juncture, it is critical to note that Jesus in His incarnate life did not have access to the full range of divine capacities that He inherently possessed in the Godhead as the eternal Word and Son of God. He willingly submitted to the conditions and limitations of the Incarnation because our salvation required that He come to earth as the Second Adam. His obedience had to be real, in that it had to be the obedience of one who was fully human. The apostle Paul shows that the Second Adam must reverse Adam's original sin to make redemption possible. "For as through the one man's disobedience the many were made sinners, even so through the obedience of the One the many will be made righteous." (Romans 5:19) Jesus was fully human as we are human, except that He knew no sin. (Hebrews 4:15)

Only because Jesus submitted to the humiliation of the Incarnation, accepting the consequences of becoming truly human, can He therefore be legitimately considered an example for those who believe in Him. This means that Jesus refused to take advantage of His inherently divine capacities that had been at His disposal forever in the Godhead. He did not violate the authentic boundaries of the human nature that became His when He emerged from His mother's womb.

Sinless Humanity is Submitted Humanity

Jesus was an authentic human, but not an independent human. He was unwilling to rely upon the resources of His own independent humanity, but only thought and did what His heavenly Father initiated through Him. That meant that the words and works of Jesus were not His own, in the sense of having their origin in His natural human mind apart from the Father's intervention. He only said and did His Father's words and works, thus all that flowed out of Jesus' life was of divine origin. As Jesus stated, "Do you not believe that I am in the Father, and the Father is in Me? The words that I say to you I do not speak on My own initiative, but the Father abiding in Me does His works." (John 14:10) The divinity that He expressed was not His inherent divinity as the Word and Son but had its source from another member of the Triune Godhead. Jesus' role as a model of desired human behavior has validity because the source of divine agency within Him, prompting and empowering Him to do the Father's works, is the Holy Spirit.

The Holy Spirit: Jesus' Source and Ours

Two issues stand out. First, all humanity needs the presence of divinity to realize life's full potential, yet divinity is not inherently present in human nature. Therefore, the divine presence needed by humanity must come from an external source. Second, Jesus modeled human life lived in the fullness of the Holy Spirit. That He qualified as a model of human dependence upon the divine presence meant that His source was not His own divinity but came from His Father's provision of the Holy Spirit, the same provision the Father makes available to any willing human recipient.

Jesus was divine, but the supernatural reality that He experienced during His earthly pilgrimage did not flow from His divine nature. The dimension of the supernatural Jesus experienced was derived from the Father's provision of the Holy Spirit. When Jesus exemplified an abundance of divine wisdom and power, He did so without violating the nature and conditions of His authentic humanity. His experience, therefore, models for us the very real possibility of being led, equipped and empowered by a source not found in our natural humanity. As we have been given the gift of the Holy Spirit, we have the privilege of tapping into the same source of the supernatural experienced by Jesus Himself.

Authentic Human Living Requires the Supernatural

This means that natural human capacity alone is unfit for the task of emulating the lifestyle of Jesus. Jesus revealed that authentic human living transcends natural capacities. Humanity was created with the capacity not only to relate to God, but to be a living receptacle of divine life. Humanity is regulated by natural conditions corresponding to finitude yet is also endowed with the capacity to receive and experience the infinite. It could be said that it is not unnatural for humans to participate in the supernatural. Humanity is made with the potential to cross back and forth into both dimensions: the natural and the supernatural. Yet the supernatural must regulate or govern the natural. Paul calls it, walking according to the Spirit (Romans 8:4). When the natural attempts to govern the supernatural, then a fleshly condition appears which grieves the Holy Spirit (Romans 8:6-8).

Jesus set an example for new born Christians in that He never allowed His Adamic nature to dominate His humanity. He made the determination that His human will would respond only to the will of His heavenly Father as revealed to Him by the Holy Spirit. When Jesus completed His redemptive mission by giving Himself up to death on the cross of Calvary, He established for all born again believers coming after Him the possibility of obeying the Spirit's directives rather than yielding to the tendencies of fleshly existence. When one is a believer, the natural realm no longer defines the boundaries of human capacity. Believers have the Spirit's presence to open up the entire realm of the supernatural unavailable to natural humanity.

Spirit Control Opens Up the Supernatural Dimension

More specifically, the believer has died to the natural realm of behavior, having identified with Jesus' cross in baptism, and has turned to the Holy Spirit to provide resources of a supernatural nature befitting the new life now unfolding under the Lordship of Jesus. Whether tasks are clearly extraordinary or are seemingly small and mundane, they take on a radically different character for the believer in that they now are accomplished through a different source. Thoughts and actions are not carried out through self-reliance, but initial submission to the Holy Spirit's control now fuels the believer's behavior. The believer's willing response is now to give way to the Spirit's presence and enablement in the exercise of a given thought or action.

Jesus Unique as Incarnate God and Savior

Only in this context is it possible to consider Jesus' extraordinary human life as a model for emulation. Of course, there are aspects of Jesus' life not meant to be emulated. Most notably, Jesus is God incarnate. He is the eternal Word and Son of God, made flesh for our sakes and our salvation. He is the unique Incarnation of God. No other person is both God and man. It is not possible, nor is it desirable, to emulate Jesus as the absolutely unique God/man. In addition, Jesus is the Jewish Messiah and Savior of the world. This unique mission was meant to be filled by Him and by no one else. He satisfied every requirement in the accomplishment of this unique mission, and His status as Messiah/Savior will never be altered. Jesus is the Jewish Messiah, and the Jews will never need another. Jesus is the world's Savior, and the world will never need another. Jesus' roles as God incarnate, as Jewish Messiah, and as the world's Savior are not open to imitation or emulation. He who would place himself in any such position either is insane or simply a deluded imposter.

We Emulate Jesus in His Total Submission to the Father

Yet other aspects of Jesus' life are meant for our emulation. As a Jew, Jesus not only abided by the standards of the Mosaic Law, but He went beyond mere legal compliance. He set forth the commandment to love God, neighbor and oneself as the summation of all that the Old Testament Law and prophets required of all who desire to do the will of God. He modeled for all who would come after Him what it meant to live in complete adherence to the supreme commandment of love. Jesus calls everyone to do as He did, in emulating His commitment to live out His life in personal relationship with His Father God, never breaking intimate communion and never straying into disobedience in word or deed. He is our model in His refusal to take self-initiative in anything but was willing to respond to the initiative of His Father in carrying out the words and works that His Father purposed for Him. And in the implementation of His Father's words and works, He never failed to give place to the Holy Spirit's presence and enablement operating through Him as the Father's divine agent of implementation.

Had Jesus done the Father's works through dependence upon His inherent divinity, then He would not have qualified to be our example. We do not, nor will we ever, have a divine nature to be the source of our words and works. But if the same Holy Spirit provided by the Father for Jesus to rely upon is also provided for us, then the possibility now exists for Jesus to be our example.

Chapter 8

Jesus as Example: Spirit Baptism

Spirit Baptism is Given for Ministry Empowerment

THE POWER COMMENSURATE with the fullness of Jesus' life, which is the desired norm for carrying out Jesus' commission for His church, comes with the baptism of the Holy Spirit. Spirit baptism, representing the initial filling of the Holy Spirit for ministry empowerment, is distinguished from the reception of the Holy Spirit at conversion, when the Holy Spirit originally enters and indwells the individual. These two phases of the Spirit's work may represent different experiences in time, or they may be received simultaneously in such a way that the recipient perceives them virtually as one experience.

Spirit Baptism May Not Be Chronologically Distinct from Conversion

Cornelius and His household seem to have experienced both phases at once, for as they responded with openness to Peter's preaching of the Gospel, the Holy Spirit both converted and empowered them almost simultaneously. (Acts 10:44-48) However, in another Acts passage, the two phases are more sharply differentiated. Paul found in Ephesus a group of twelve men who had received the baptism of John the Baptist. After Paul explained to them the Gospel, they believed in Jesus and were baptized in His name. Immediately following their conversion, Paul then laid His hands upon them to receive the baptism of the Holy Spirit. The Scripture notes, "the Holy Spirit came on them, and they began speaking with tongues and prophesying." (Acts 19:6) In this case, the time differential was brief. In other cases, a much longer period can separate an individual's initial reception of the Holy Spirit at conversion from the experience of empowerment that comes with Spirit baptism.

Clear Logical Distinction

The two phases may or may not be set apart in time, which is a chronological distinction. But the primary consideration is not chronological but logical. According to the New Testament, a logical distinction exists between the impartation of the Spirit at conversion and the Spirit's impartation releasing empowerment. The biblical events that establish the logical distinctions of these two impartations are worthy of consideration in this context.

Post Resurrection Appearance

The conversion of humanity awaited the successful completion of Jesus' redemptive work. As Jesus' gave up unto death His human spirit on the cross, thereby completing His part in the prophetic fulfillment of redemption, the Father confirmed the atoning merit of His Son's death by raising Him from the grave to be the firstborn of a new redeemed humanity that eventually will share Jesus' resurrected and immortal humanity. For a designated period of forty days, the resurrected Jesus remained on earth revealing Himself to His disciples. A pivotal moment arrived when Jesus first encountered His disciples as a group on the night of His resurrection. After greeting them, Jesus established His identity by showing them the wounds of His crucifixion.

The Disciples' Initial Reception of the Spirit
After challenging and comforting them with His words, Jesus climaxed the event by initiating a moment of impartation that would alter forever the nature of relationship between God and humanity. Jesus "breathed on them, and said to them, 'Receive the Holy Spirit." (John 20:22) As the Lord God first created humanity by breathing "into his (Adam's) nostrils the breath of life," (Genesis 2:7) so the resurrected Jesus recreated sinful humanity by His breath. The new birth, essential to eternal life, now became available to all who would believe. As His disciples believed on Him that day as the resurrected Lord of life, the Holy Spirit came to dwell in them forever.

Over the three-year span of time the disciples spent with Jesus during His public ministry, they had enjoyed the accompaniment of the Holy Spirit often. But now, the Holy Spirit came to dwell in them permanently, as freshly born babes of the new creation. (II Corinthians 5:17) Prior to His crucifixion, Jesus had predicted this moment. "And I will ask the Father, and He will give you another Helper, that He may be with you forever; that is the Spirit of truth, whom the world cannot receive, because it does not behold Him or know Him, but you know Him because He abides with you, and **will be in you**." (John 14:16-17)

More to Accomplish After Redemption

The ushering in of the new birth undoubtedly was the single most pivotal event in human history, apart from which no human being would ever see the kingdom of God (John 3:3) Completing the redemptive phase of His mission, the resurrected Jesus now freely offered His abundant, eternal life to all who would receive Him. (John 1:12) Yet Jesus' redemptive triumph propelled Him into other phases of His purpose not possible until the new birth had become available.

Jesus: Baptizer in the Holy Spirit

The most critical function assumed by Jesus after bestowing the new birth was to fulfill His role as baptizer in the Holy Spirit. Every Gospel writer repeated the announcement by John the Baptist that the Messiah would come baptizing in the Holy Spirit. (Matthew 3:11, Mark 1:8, Luke 3:16, John 1:33) The New Testament is clear that the disciples' baptism of the Holy Spirit was a decidedly different experience than their reception of the Holy Spirit for the new birth. (John 20:22) Spirit baptism is identified as a bestowal of empowerment, equipping believers for their mission that requires supernatural enablement. After receiving their commission, the disciples were instructed by Jesus not to go forth immediately, but to go to Jerusalem to wait until they became "clothed with power from on high." (Luke 24:49)

Spirit Baptism Not Given Until the Day of Pentecost
Jesus reiterated His instructions on the day that He ascended to heaven. "And gathering them together, He commanded them not to leave Jerusalem, but to wait for what the Father had promised, 'Which,' He said, 'you heard of from Me; for John baptized with water, but you shall be baptized with the Holy Spirit not many days from now.'" He continued, "...but you shall receive power when the Holy Spirit has come upon you; and you shall be My witnesses ... even to the remotest part of the earth." (Acts 1:4-5, 8) It was on the Day of Pentecost, while the disciples were in a Jerusalem room together in prayer, that they received their baptism of power. A noise from heaven like a violent, rushing wind filled the house where the disciples were waiting. Tongues of fire appeared, resting on each of the 120 members of Jesus' church. All were filled with the Holy Spirit, and they "began to speak with other tongues, as the Spirit was giving them utterance." (Acts 2:2-4) They flooded into the Jerusalem streets, continuing to articulate their unintelligible uttering. To

their amazement, people from various nations were able to understand what they were saying. "... we hear them in our own tongues speaking of the mighty deeds of God." (Acts 2:11)

The Commission Requires Supernatural Power

A crowd gathered, and Peter rose to preach. He identified the supernatural experience being observed by the people as the baptism of the Holy Spirit coming from the ascended Jesus in heaven. "Therefore having been exalted to the right hand of God, and having received from the Father the promise of the Holy Spirit, He has poured forth this which you both see and hear." (Acts 2:33) Undoubtedly, nothing less than power from on high would suffice to arm the disciples to accomplish the specific task laid out by Jesus prior to His ascension. "And He said to them, 'Go into all the world and preach the gospel to all creation. He who has believed and has been baptized shall be saved; but he who has disbelieved shall be condemned. And these signs will accompany those who have believed: in My name they will cast out demons, they will speak with new tongues; they will pick up serpents, and if they drink any deadly poison, it shall not hurt them; they will lay hands on the sick, and they will recover.'" (Mark 16:15-18) Only the baptism of the Holy Spirit, conveying the Father's promise of power from on high, could open up for the disciples the miraculous dimension required by Jesus' commission.

After Pentecost, Proclamation Without Power

More than twenty centuries later, that same commission still stands as a mandate for the church. Yet most of those centuries have come and gone with generations of Christians attempting to accomplish their commission without the supernatural resources of Spirit baptism. This means that most of the church's history has found the church engaging in the evangelistic enterprise without the attesting supernatural signs of the Holy Spirit. Jesus forbade His earliest disciples to go forth in evangelization without the reception of Spirit baptism. Yet generation after generation of Christians has ventured forth in evangelism without the necessary clothing of "power from on high." They have trusted in proclamation without power, a practice with absolutely no Scriptural foundation. When the ascended Jesus poured forth the baptism in the Spirit upon His original disciples, He established a pattern of ministry intended to be followed by every succeeding generation of believers. "And they went out and preached everywhere, while the Lord worked with them, and confirmed the word by the signs that followed." (Mark 16:20)

Jesus Is Still the Baptizer

Jesus set a precedent for normative church life by assuming His role in heaven as the baptizer in the Holy Spirit. He has never relinquished that role. He is just as desirous today as He was on the Day of Pentecost to pour forth "the Father's promise" of "power from on high" upon any yielded, submitted believer. Because Jesus Himself is baptizer in the Holy Spirit, no believer should refuse to be baptized in the Spirit's power. It simply is a matter of obeying Jesus' plan for the implementation of the Great Commission in the earth.

Chapter 9

Jesus as Example: Receiver of the Spirit

Source of Miracles

CHRISTIAN OPINION FOR TOO LONG has falsely hoisted Jesus onto a pedestal by attributing the miracles that He performed to His divine majesty. Although Jesus deserves all of our praise for His legacy of miraculous works, we are not detracting from the praise that He is due because we recognize that His miracles were accomplished through the Spirit's anointing upon Him. That He ministered so powerfully without relying upon the resources of His own divine nature is an accomplishment of far greater magnitude than had He insisted upon utilizing His divinity.

Pattern for the Church

Furthermore, by doing miraculous works in the weakness of His humanity, while depending upon the Spirit's power, Jesus was demonstrating to His disciples how His supernatural ministry should be continued when He would no longer be physically present. If Jesus depended upon the Spirit to do miraculous works, so can we. If Christians view Jesus' supernatural works as setting a pattern for what the church is to accomplish, then faith is increased within the church to follow through with the challenge of the Great Commission. Incentive is diminished when believers face a daunting assignment with no confidence that supernatural assistance is available. To applaud Jesus for His supernatural ministry, while believing that we are powerless to do similar works, affords Him no glory.

Jesus, Both Giver and Receiver of the Holy Spirit

The same Jesus who stepped into His role as Baptizer of the Holy Spirit on the Day of Pentecost is the One who received and depended upon the Holy Spirit in His incarnate humanity. Giver of the Holy Spirit as God, Jesus also received the Holy Spirit when He became human for the sake of human redemption. Since Jesus' humanity was real, and not augmented by the attributes of His divinity, Jesus' dependence upon the presence and resources of the Holy Spirit were real. We see in the human Jesus, living in the fullness and anointing of the Holy Spirit, a pattern of life as it was meant to be lived in the condition of the Spirit's indwelling and anointing.

Modeled Complete Submission to the Spirit

Jesus lived out His incarnate life with this purpose in mind. He intended for His human existence to be a pattern for His church of what it means to live life in complete submission and compliance with the operations of the Holy Spirit. The apostle John understood the relevance of Jesus' human life for the church. "... as He is, so also are we in this world." (I John 4:17) This is true, both in sanctification and in empowerment.

Sanctification by the Spirit

Jesus kept Himself separated from sin not by means of inherent holiness but by yielding completely to the Spirit's control. The Spirit's sanctifying presence is always available to minister to humanity the standards of righteousness. Jesus' personal holiness was maintained on that basis. Jesus stated in John's Gospel, "And for their sakes I sanctify Myself, that they themselves also may be sanctified in truth." (John 17:19)

Anointing of Power by the Spirit

Furthermore, Jesus' anointing of power exemplified in His public ministry was not derived from His inherent divinity but from His total yieldedness to the Spirit's anointing. On various occasions, Jesus gave authority and power to His disciples to work miracles even before the Spirit was released to indwell them permanently. (e.g., Luke 9:1-2) He was preparing them for what would come later, after their baptism in the Holy Spirit, when their lives and ministries would be characterized by the supernatural gifts, signs and wonders of the Spirit. Jesus taught His disciples to expect a lifestyle of the Spirit's anointing. "Truly, truly, I say to you, he who believes in Me, the works that I do shall he do also; and greater works than these shall he do; because I go to the Father." (John 14:12) Jesus fully intended that His life of sanctification and power be reproduced by those coming after Him, for the Spirit that filled His humanity would also fill them.

The solid Scriptural foundation for asserting that Jesus' power was derived from the Holy Spirit and not from His inherent divinity deserves further consideration. Traditionally, scholars have skewed the Scriptural perspective of the Spirit's major role in Jesus' life and ministry because of their exaggerated emphasis upon Jesus' divinity. Excessively defensive in response to liberal trends attempting to rob Jesus of His divinity, scholars have failed to embrace the full implications of the doctrine of the Incarnation.

The Spirit's Role in Jesus' Conception

Interestingly, these scholars see no threat in recognizing the Spirit's significant place in Jesus' origins. They view Jesus' unique origin to be the result of His miraculous conception in the womb of Mary by the seed of the Holy Spirit. As recorded by Luke, the angel Gabriel revealed to Mary how Jesus would be conceived. "'And behold, you will conceive in your womb, and bear a son, and you shall name Him Jesus.' ...And Mary said to the angel, 'How can this be, since I am a virgin?' And the angel answered and said to her, 'The Holy Spirit will come upon you, and the power of the Most High will overshadow you; and for that reason the holy offspring shall be called the Son of God.'" (Luke 1:31, 34-35) By placing weight upon the Spirit's role in Jesus' miraculous conception, these scholars are reinforcing Jesus' divine identity. If He was conceived by the Holy Spirit, rather than through natural origins, Jesus' preexistence as God's eternal Son can be defended.

Jettisoning of the Spirit

Once Jesus' supernatural conception is established, these scholars are ready to jettison the Spirit's role in Jesus' sanctification and empowerment, attributing sole responsibility to His inherent divinity. The Scriptural record does not corroborate this interpretation. Wrongly crediting works accomplished through the Spirit's enablement to the inherent power of Jesus' divinity leads to faulty Christological and theological conclusions that have far reaching consequences for Christian living.

John's Insight

Much error may have been avoided had Christian scholarship faithfully interpreted the apostle John's pivotal passage revealing the Father's abundant provision of the Spirit bestowed upon Jesus. Not only had Jesus been born uniquely by the Spirit's conception in His mother Mary, but, as John appropriately indicated, Jesus was endowed with the Spirit's fullness from His conception onwards.[11]

---

[11] This Scriptural phrase conveys a double meaning; "… for He gives the Spirit without measure." (vs. 34) 1) This refers to the Father's bountiful provision of the Holy Spirit to His people in a general sense.

(John 3:34-35) Jesus was provided with the full measure of the Holy Spirit at His conception in His mother's womb, not as a luxury, but of absolute necessity. The reality of His Incarnation required that Jesus' frail, mortal humanity be sustained by the Spirit's sanctifying, empowering presence.

Developing Consciousness of the Spirit's Role

Since the incarnate Jesus did not have the benefit of His omniscient divinity, He was required to develop consciousness of His messianic identity and purpose. His growth and learning were according to patterns of human development. "The Child continued to grow and become strong, increasing in wisdom; and the grace of God was upon Him… And Jesus kept increasing in wisdom and stature, and in favor with God and men." (Luke 2:40, 52) Jesus would have become aware of the prominent place of the Spirit in His life by recognizing that key messianic passages in the Old Testament were meant to be fulfilled by Him. Isaiah prophetically foretold that Jehovah God would put His Spirit upon the Messiah. "Behold, My Servant, whom I uphold; My chosen one in whom My soul delights. I have put My Spirit upon Him; He will bring forth justice to the nations." (Isaiah 42:1) In Matthew's Gospel, this specific prophecy is appropriated personally

---

2) More specifically, this phrase refers to the Father's provision of the Holy Spirit given without measure to Jesus. Verse 35 confirms the reference to Jesus in this context, when it is said, "The Father loves the Son, and has given all things into His hand."

by Jesus, indicating that He knew that the Spirit was upon Him. "But Jesus, … healed them all, and warned them not to tell who He was. This was to fulfill what was spoken through Isaiah the prophet: 'Behold, My servant whom I have chosen; My Beloved in whom My soul is well pleased; **I will put My Spirit upon Him**, and He shall proclaim justice to the Gentiles.'" (Matthew 12:15-18)

Another prominent prophetic passage from Isaiah figured directly in the formation of Jesus' self-understanding. "**The Spirit of the Lord God is upon me**, because **the Lord has anointed me** to bring good news to the afflicted; He has sent me to bind up the brokenhearted, to proclaim liberty to captives and freedom to prisoners;" (Isaiah 61:1) Jesus chose the correct moment while reading this passage in the synagogue in His hometown of Nazareth to disclose publicly that He was the anointed One to whom Isaiah was referring. "He entered the synagogue on the Sabbath, and stood up to read. And the book of the prophet Isaiah was handed to Him. And He opened the book and found the place where it was written, '**The Spirit of the Lord is upon Me**, because **He anointed me** to preach to the poor. He sent Me to proclaim release to the captives,' … And He closed the book, gave it back to the attendant and sat down; and the eyes of all in the synagogue were fixed on Him. And He began to say to them, 'Today this Scripture has been fulfilled in your hearing.'" (Luke 4:16-21) Jesus seized this opportunity to declare publicly, not only that

He was aware that the Spirit's anointing would rest upon the Messiah, but that He Himself was that very Messiah.

From Indwelling to Spirit-baptism

Timing was extremely important in the providential unfolding of the phases of Jesus' messianic purpose. For instance, Jesus had been filled with the Spirit while in the womb of His mother. Yet He waited until He was thirty years of age on the occasion of His water baptism by John the Baptist to appropriate the supernatural power that would accompany His public ministry. Prior to that point, we are not aware of any miracles performed by Jesus. The Spirit's anointing of power that characterized the three years of His public ministry was not manifested until His water baptism. This division of the Spirit's operations in Jesus would have implications for the redeemed company coming after Him. 1) The Spirit's entrance and fullness established in Jesus' life from His conception in the womb is equated with the experience of the new birth in the life of the Christian. The Spirit's sanctifying presence and influence in Jesus' humanity was initiated at His conception. Likewise, the Spirit takes the commanding role in the life of the believer at the moment of conversion. 2) Jesus needed the Spirit's supernatural anointing to confirm His proclamation of the coming of God's kingdom when He began His public ministry. Jesus' anointing corresponds with the occasion of Spirit baptism in the believer's life, releasing supernatural signs and wonders to confirm the preaching of the Gospel to every nation under heaven. Every Christian has some role in the fulfillment of the Great Commission. The Spirit's indwelling occurring at the moment of conversion is not enough to meet the demands of Jesus' mandate. Spirit baptism is the subsequent step after conversion to equip every believer with the supernatural resources needed to fulfill their task.

Supernatural Anointing

Nowhere in the New Testament do we see Jesus asserting His divinity in the carrying out of His mission. Instead, through the years of His public ministry, Jesus yielded fully to His Father's provision of the Holy Spirit. The influence of divinity never left Him, yet the source of supernatural power that He ever relied upon was the Holy Spirit. A statement in Peter's sermon to the Gentiles, recorded by Luke, leaves no question as to the source of Jesus' power. "You know of Jesus of Nazareth, how God anointed Him with the Holy Spirit and with power, and how He went about doing good and healing all who were oppressed by the devil, for God was with Him." (Acts 10:38)

Frail Humanity and the Spirit

Jesus continually required supernatural power in overcoming Satan's strategies, and in releasing people from Satan's bondage. Yet the ultimate release, eternal redemption for Adam's race, could not be won by an exclusively divine being. Only incarnate divinity, the Second Adam, could reverse the curse by sinless obedience and atoning sacrifice. His divinity held in check, Jesus won by His human reliance upon the Holy Spirit. The Father's power was manifest in His victory, but not through His inherent resources as God's Son. Jesus won in frail, mortal humanity, ever yielding to the control of the Holy Spirit made available to Him. Luke registers the pervasive influence exercised by the Holy Spirit upon the incarnate Jesus. "Jesus, full of the Holy Spirit, returned from the Jordan and was led around by the Spirit in the wilderness ..." "And Jesus returned to Galilee in the power of the Spirit, and news about Him spread through all the surrounding district." (Luke 4:1, 14) In another reference, Matthew reveals the source of His successful assault against Satan's kingdom. "But if I cast out demons by the Spirit of God, then the kingdom of God has come upon you." (Matthew 12:28)

His Anointing is for the Church

The New Testament witness is sufficiently clear to indicate that the source of power operative in Jesus is the same source of power dispensed by Jesus upon His church on the Day of Pentecost. The source of power received by Jesus in His incarnate humanity is the same source of power into which He baptized His church as He equipped His believers with the power to carry out the Great Commission. The source of anointing exemplified in His public ministry is intended to be operative in the lives of all who identify with His name. As Jesus went about the land proclaiming the kingdom of God, He needed the accompaniment and confirmation of the Spirit's gifts, signs and wonders. Those same gifts, signs and wonders also are needed as Jesus' church continues to proclaim the Gospel to needy world.

In summation, Jesus experienced phases of the Spirit's presence and power in His own humanity in order to prepare the way for the coming operations of the Spirit in the lives of believers. Had Jesus found the source of power for ministry in His own divine nature, His own people would have been powerless in life and ministry, for only Jesus could claim natural divinity as God's only Son. Therefore, Jesus' freely relinquished the privileges of His divinity and humbly submitted to the lowly conditions of Adam's estate for the sake of His church. Jesus relied upon the only source of power made available to Him, the Father's impartation of the Holy Spirit. Allowing His humanity to become a channel for the Spirit's power, Jesus obediently fulfilled His purpose by bringing salvation to Adam's race.

Demonstration of the Spirit and Power

Jesus' ministry of healing, deliverance and reconciliation among the people set a precedent for the church coming after Him. As He had been sent by the Father, He sent forth His church to transmit His Gospel to all nations. As the ascended Lord, the source of His power now could be imparted to them. On the Day of Pentecost, Jesus baptized His church with the same anointing of the Spirit's presence

He had known for three years of public ministry. Although weak in His flesh, Jesus had healed the sick, opened the eyes of the blind, loosed the tongues of the dumb, driven demons from the oppressed, and even raised the dead to life. This unparalleled expression of the supernatural was not intended by Jesus to be simply an historical legacy, but a pattern of ministry duplicated by His church where ever His name and Spirit are present. The baptism of the Spirit imparted by Jesus upon the early church was never rescinded but represents a continuous reservoir of spiritual life and power available to every generation of believers who will partake. Jesus never intended His Gospel to be transmitted in word only but conveyed to a needy world in demonstration of the Spirit and power. Our role is not to imitate His actions as we remember His deeds, but to participate with Him as He continues to minister to people in the mighty power of the Spirit. Willing vessels free to be used are those submitted to the baptism of the Holy Spirit. No more glorious occupation has ever graced God's children than to be a habitation of the Holy Spirit.

Chapter 10

Jesus as Example: Empowerment

New Testament Emphasis

THE ROLE OF JESUS as Baptizer in the Holy Spirit holds a place of emphasis in the New Testament that is not maintained consistently in Christian history. John the Baptist heralded Jesus as the One who had come to baptize the people in the Holy Spirit and fire, a function implemented only after Jesus had become the risen, ascended Lord. The first official act fulfilled by Jesus after His ascension was to discharge His role as Baptizer in the Holy Spirit. The purpose of Spirit baptism was not to impart the Spirit to the unconverted. Spirit baptism was an additional phase of impartation. His church needed supernatural endowments of power to take the Gospel to the uttermost parts of the earth. Mere human ability and ingenuity would not be sufficient. Jesus never intended for ministry to be attempted without the supernatural provision of the Spirit's baptism.

Lacking Empowerment

Jesus' disciples would seem to have been prepared for ministry prior to His ascension. After all, they had passed through some major experiences since Jesus' death on the cross. First, the disciples had regathered following news of Jesus' resurrection. Then their personal encounter with the risen Christ occurred. In that event, they received the Holy Spirit, becoming new born members of His church.[12] Following their conversion and establishment as His church, they received His commission to take the Gospel to the nations of the world. Yet despite the passage these events, they were not ready to undertake their ministry. Jesus' strategy had not been revealed in full.

While in the company of His church on the day of His ascension, Jesus gave them clear instructions to return to Jerusalem to pray and wait for the Father's promise of Spirit baptism to come upon them. His church obeyed. Within a few days, while the church was gathered in prayer on the Day of Pentecost, the climactic event took place. Every member of the church received the baptism of the Holy Spirit. That very day, the church took to the streets to preach the Gospel to the various people groups assembled in Jerusalem. The power from on high had been sent from Jesus above, equipping believers with

---

[12] Jesus' resurrection signaled the completion of His redemptive work. He appeared to His disciples immediately following His resurrection to substantiate His identity and to breathe upon them the regenerative life of the Holy Spirit (John 20:22).

supernatural gifts, signs and wonders to accompany their ministry to others.

Precise Strategy
These critical events in the life of Jesus reveal a precise strategy for His ongoing ministry through His church. Certain logical conclusions may be ventured as we examine His strategy. It seems clear that Jesus logically separated the Spirit's work of regeneration from the Spirit's work of empowerment. In the first distinct work of the Spirit in the individual, the Spirit converts the recipient into a new creation inhabited by the Holy Spirit. In the second distinct work, the Spirit overflows the new believer with power, equipping the recipient with supernatural gifts for ministry. Jesus is unequivocal in His strategy to separate logically these distinct operations of the Holy Spirit.

Dual Operations of the Spirit
Because the Spirit's dual operations target different functions, it is more common for these experiences to be separated chronologically. Both experiences usually result in radical change for the individual, but different in kind. The Spirit's work of conversion transforms the individual from a life of self-centeredness and separation from God into an intimate relationship with God that radically alters motives and perceptions. With an entirely new worldview coming into focus, the new believer often is not yet aware of the need to receive the Spirit's power for ministry.

Spirit Baptism is a Logically Distinct Experience

Following the New Testament pattern, as the believer's new identity becomes solidified, the responsibility to minister the Gospel to others should come into focus. Jesus' strategy recognizes the absolute necessity of equipping the believer in the Spirit's supernatural power before venturing into ministry. That additional impartation of the Spirit's power beyond conversion is the baptism of the Holy Spirit. This impartation makes available to the believer a variety of supernatural resources both for personal edification, for ministry to fellow believers, and ministry to persons who have yet to receive Christ. Therefore, because the Spirit's workings in conversion are quite distinct from the Spirit's endowment of power, it is common for believers to experience Spirit baptism as a chronologically separate event from conversion, although a separation in time is not mandatory.[13] Critical to this discussion, however, is the

---

[13] An exceptional case is the experience of Cornelius and his household, recorded in chapter ten of the Acts of the Apostles. God sent Peter to preach to them, their first exposure to the Gospel of Jesus Christ. Before Peter could complete his message, the Holy Spirit came upon the entire group. Not only did they believe in the Gospel, bringing the Spirit's regeneration into their lives, but simultaneously they received the Spirit's power. Here, no chronological separation occurred between the reception of the Spirit imparting regeneration and the reception of the Spirit's power, evidenced by the utterances of tongues speech coming from the newly converted. Generally, such cases are the exception rather than the rule. For most people, a chronological as well as a logical separation occurs in the Spirit's dual operations.

requirement to adhere to Jesus' complete strategy of allowing for two logically distinct operations of the Spirit. To stop at conversion, without extending the mandate of Christ to receive the baptism of the Holy Spirit, results in a deficient Christian experience and church life. Jesus wants the ministry of His church in the earth to be the product of the miraculous power of God. He does not want His church to represent simply the best of human ingenuity and effort, but to reveal the glory and power of God.

The Spirit's Distinct Workings in Jesus' Incarnate Life

When Jesus' pattern of the Spirit's operations is understood, other aspects of the Spirit's work as revealed in the New Testament follow this logical development. Jesus' personal life fits the pattern. We know that at Jesus' conception in the womb of His mother, the Spirit came to inhabit Him and to assist Him to do the will of His heavenly Father. For thirty years, the Spirit's sanctifying presence enabled Jesus to live without sin, even though His humanity was the frail, finite human nature common to Adam's race. Yet when the appointed time arrived for Jesus' to launch out in public ministry, He was visited with a special anointing of the Spirit on the occasion of His baptism at the hands of John the Baptist. We have no record of Jesus preaching or performing miracles until after this special anointing of the Spirit's power.

Jesus' Conception is our New Birth; His Anointing is our Spirit Baptism

Two distinct operations of the Spirit in Jesus' life provide for us a clearer understanding of the pattern of the Spirit's work in the believer. Jesus' conception is analogous to the conversion of the believer, when the Spirit is received to regenerate and sanctify the individual. Yet Jesus gave His church a commission to fulfill, to make disciples of the nations of the world. The Spirit's supernatural power is needed for such a task. The baptism of the Spirit clothes the believer with power from on high, equipping each member with giftings of the Spirit that are miraculous in nature. Spirit baptism for the believer is equated with the descent of the Spirit upon Jesus at His baptism, anointing Him with the Spirit's miraculous power to prepare Him to embark upon His public ministry.

One Coming, but Two Operations of the Spirit
These two distinct workings of the Spirit are not to be understood as receiving the Holy Spirit twice. Jesus was given the Holy Spirit only once, at the moment of His conception. From that point forward, Jesus always had the presence of the Holy Spirit within Him. Yet at His baptism, He was visited with an anointing of that same Holy Spirit, enabling Him to utilize supernatural giftings in the exercise of His ministry to people. Believers also receive the Holy Spirit only once, when the Spirit comes to bring conversion. Yet at Spirit baptism, believers are activated by the Spirit's anointing. They are thus equipped to go forth in ministry to people with supernatural giftings of the Spirit.

Spirit Baptism Benefits Church as well as World

Not only an unconverted world benefits from the church's baptism in the Spirit, but the individual members receive ministry from the charismata imparted to the congregation. When the local church is assembled together, individuals are given a variety of gifts to benefit one another. Each member is not given all the gifts, so that individuals can learn to depend upon each other as the Spirit distributes diverse giftings throughout the membership. Special mention, however, should be made in reference to the gift of tongues. Like other spiritual manifestations, tongues is meant to be expressed only through a few individuals when the local assembly is gathered together. Tongues messages are to be spoken sparingly, and only when members are present who exercise the gift of interpretation of tongues that must accompany the gift of tongues in a public gathering.

Jesus' Strategy: The Gift of Tongues for Every Believer

The gift of speaking in tongues is exceptional, however, in that it is a gift given to every Christian who receives the baptism in the Holy Spirit. That is because speaking in tongues functions first in the believer's experience as an initial sign of the reception of the Spirit's baptism. The Acts of the Apostles records that all 120 believers assembled in the Upper Room on the Day of Pentecost spoke in tongues as the sign that the baptism in the Holy Spirit had been released from heaven through Jesus' impartation. On another significant occasion, as Peter was assigned to preach to Cornelius' household, the first expansion of the Gospel to non-Jewish peoples, the Spirit's baptism fell upon every single family member at once while Peter was delivering his sermon. Peter later reported to the Jerusalem church that he had confidence that the Gentiles in Cornelius' house truly had been baptized in the Holy Spirit, because they were given the same gift of tongues that had been visited upon the original disciples on the Day of Pentecost. (Acts 11:15-18) Another event is recorded in the Acts of the Apostles that reveals Spirit baptism being received, with tongues speech being expressed by every recipient. Paul encountered twelve Ephesians, ministered the Gospel to them, baptized them in water, and laid hands upon them to receive Spirit baptism. "…the Holy Spirit came upon them, and they began speaking with tongues and prophesying." (Acts 19:6) In conclusion, since the Great Commission to communicate the Gospel to a lost world is a mandate for every believer, and ministry necessitates the equipping of power from on high through Spirit baptism, it follows that every believer needs the baptism in the Holy Spirit. Since the gift of tongues functions initially in the believer's experience as the sign that Spirit baptism has been received, it is logical to infer that Jesus strategically planned for every believer to receive the gift of tongues.

The Pattern from Paul's Ministry

Further evidence from the New Testament may be garnered from Paul's first letter to the Corinthians. His chief concern in chapter fourteen is to restore order to an unruly congregation who had fallen into the practice of allowing tongues speech to be voiced too frequently, and without following those utterances with accompanying interpretations of the tongues messages. While providing necessary correction, Paul also reveals important insights concerning tongues as a gift of the Spirit. Paul makes two statements that indicate the high value that he personally places on this gift, while expressing his desire that all believers possess the gift. "I thank God I speak in tongues more than you all;" (verse 18) and "I wish that you all spoke in tongues, ..." (verse 5) Were it not the will of God for all to speak with other tongues, it would not be likely that Paul would state in Scripture his desire for that occurrence.

Tongues Given for Self-edification
Another statement lends further credence to this conclusion. Prior to expressing his desire that all believers speak in tongues, Paul notes, that "one who speaks in a tongue edifies himself." (verse 4) A previous verse augments the significance of that statement. "For one who speaks in a tongue does not speak to men, but to God; for no one understands, but in his spirit he speaks mysteries." (verse 2) It may be inferred from these statements that speaking in tongues is a form of personal prayer that provides spiritual benefit for the speaker. Would it be

conceivable that God would play favorites by providing a special prayer language as a means of self-edification only to select members of His church rather than offering to each member of His church the privilege of utilizing this special language of prayer? After identifying tongues as a form of prayer that builds up the believer, Paul follows by asserting that he desires for every believer to experience this gift.

Tongues is Not a Spiritual Seizure

It is relevant to note in this context that Paul emphasizes the responsibility of the individual believer to exercise self-control in the expression of the gift of tongues. Throughout Christian history, persons have mistakenly believed that tongues was an ecstatic, emotionally-incited experience, seizing the recipient's vocal chords and gushing forth with strange utterances while the speaker remains in a trance-like state. While some historical accounts seem to conform to such a scenario, this description fails to align with the definitive New Testament explanation providing detailed insight as to how this gift is expected to operate in a Scriptural manner.

Paul Views Tongues as a Form of Prayer

Paul makes it unquestionably clear that tongues is simply a form of prayer that is to be uttered in essentially the same manner as one would pray with understanding. He says, "For if I pray in a tongue, my spirit prays, but my mind is unfruitful." (verse 14) Speaking in tongues is praying, but without intellectual comprehension of the content of the prayer. He goes on to say, "What is the outcome then? I shall pray with the spirit and I shall pray with the mind also; I shall sing with the spirit and I shall sing with the mind also." (verse 15) Paul is saying that the same kind of choice is involved for the believer, whether he or she prays with the spirit (speaking in tongues) or prays with the mind (with the understanding). He notes that the same is true also when one sings, whether in the spirit (with tongues) or with the mind (with understanding). Whether praying or singing in tongues, the believer is expected by Paul to exercise the same kind of control as is practiced when one prays or sings with understanding.

Restraint in the Assembly
Furthermore, Paul addresses the case when the believer is in the public assembly of the local church with no one to interpret his or her tongues speech. He instructs for the believer to remain publicly silent, "and let him speak to himself and to God." (verse 28) It is obvious that if tongues speech is an uncontrollable utterance, a "spiritual seizure" of some sort, then the tongues speaker would be without the power to refrain from exercising the gift when the urge was present, whether in public or in private. Yet Paul instructs that when the tongues speaker knows that one with the gift of interpretation is not present in the assembly, the speaker is to maintain self-control, and pray in tongues only in a private setting.

Human Volition in the Initial Reception

Even when the believer is speaking in tongues for the very first time in the experience of Spirit baptism, the utterance requires the consent of the speaker to vocalize syllables emerging from deep within his/her spirit. When the early church first experienced Spirit baptism on the Day of Pentecost, they "began to speak with other tongues as the Spirit was giving them utterance." (Acts 2:4) It should be noted that the Holy Spirit within them was giving them unintelligible syllables for them to utter, but the act of speaking was their responsibility and under their control. The Spirit gave the utterance, but they did the speaking.

Worship that Transcends and Humbles the Intellect

We have seen that tongues is a form of prayer. More specifically, tongues is an expression of worship so utterly pure and primordial that its meaning transcends conceptual comprehension. As the speaker yields consent to voice this deep form of praise to God, the indwelling Holy Spirit infuses the entire being of the speaker with supernatural power. The utterances are spoken as an act of faith, a total surrender of the voice and tongue to syllables unknown to the intellect. The pride of human intelligence must bow in submission to incomprehensible babblings believed to be the humble articulations of a completely yielded vessel.

Taming the Tongue

James reveals that the person who pleases God perfectly is able to control the tongue. The one who can control the tongue can control all of his actions. (James 3:2) Yet he laments that "no one can tame the tongue; it is a restless evil and full of deadly poison." (verse 8) When the pride of godless humanity in early civilization overstepped permitted boundaries, and the people designed a city with a tower that they intended to reach to heaven (Tower of Babel), God stepped in to put a stop to their prideful ambition. They had been one people with the same language. God said, "Come, let Us go down and there confuse their language, that they may not understand one another's speech." (Genesis 11:7) After their language was confused, they were scattered abroad over the face of the earth, and they stopped building the city. (verses 8-9) How fitting that when God finished His redemptive work in Jesus Christ, He gave His redeemed community a "new tongue," (Mark 16:17) a universal language in the Holy Spirit to unite His people in the presence and power of Jesus Christ!

Today's Mandate

Jesus and Paul have revealed a comprehensive pattern for individual and corporate experience that must be heeded if normative Christian living is to occur. Jesus' role as Spirit baptizer must be heeded, entreating every believer with the mandate to receive the supernatural impartation of Spirit baptism as a necessary preparation for effective Christian life and ministry. Every believer is responsible for receiving the resources Jesus' imparts in Spirit baptism: self-edification, corporate participation and ministry penetration. Speaking in tongues is not an optional gift accompanying Spirit baptism but is both an initial sign of the baptism's reception, as well as a new language of prayer bringing personal edification that ignites participation in the supernatural dimension on a continuous basis. Like praying in the language of one's understanding, praying in the language of the Spirit is a controlled action free to occur whenever the speaker is willing. When contemporary Christianity rediscovers and implements the biblical pattern concerning Jesus as Baptizer in the Holy Spirit and the Pauline revelation concerning speaking in tongues, revival will ignite the church with lasting reformation looming on the horizon.

Chapter 11

Jesus as Example: Speaking in Tongues

Jesus: Master Plan

JESUS WAS NO STRANGER to the experience of speaking in tongues. He announced to His followers as He was preparing them for their future mission that one of the signs to be expected among new converts would be that "they will speak with new tongues." (Mark 16:17) After completing His redemptive work and ascending to heaven, Jesus as Baptizer in the Holy Spirit poured forth upon His church the anointing of the Spirit to empower them for their mission. As this baptism descended upon the faithful, the first noticeable sign of their reception was the experience of speaking in tongues.[14] It is highly improbable that the reigning Lord responsible for this

---

[14] Tongues speech was the obvious initial manifestation exhibited by the early believers on the Day of Pentecost when Jesus first exercised His role as Baptizer in the Holy Spirit. "And there appeared to them tongues as of fire distributing themselves, and they rested on each one of them. And they were all filled with the Holy Spirit and began to speak with other tongues, as the Spirit was giving them utterance." (Acts 2:3-4)

infilling would have been surprised at the manifestation of tongues visited upon the upper room disciples on that momentous day. Especially, in view of the fact that the tongues visitation on the Day of Pentecost was not just a one-time event, but became a usual occurrence whenever believers were baptized in the Spirit,[15] adds to the probability that tongues speech from the start had been a part of Jesus' master plan to equip His people with power for life and ministry.

New Testament Pattern

Tongues speech functioned in the New Testament era both as an initial sign of the Spirit's empowerment and as a gift of worshipful utterance both for personal and corporate edification. We believe that Jesus established this pattern for His people following His resurrection and intended for

---

[15] Among other prominent Biblical accounts of tongues speech being the initial manifestation when believers received their baptism in the Holy Spirit, two are worthy of mention. 1) Pentecostal baptism was extended to the non-Jewish world for the first time when Peter was sent to Caesarea to preach the Gospel of Jesus to the household of Cornelius. "While Peter was still speaking these words, the Holy Spirit fell upon all those who were listening to the message. All the circumcised believers who came with Peter were amazed, because the gift of the Holy Spirit had been poured out on the Gentiles also. For they were hearing them speaking with tongues and exalting God." (Acts 10:44-46) 2) Paul found in Ephesus twelve men who had been disciples of John the Baptist, but who had not heard of the Gospel of Jesus. After Paul's instruction, they believed in Jesus and submitted to baptism as new converts. Paul then led them into the baptism of the Holy Spirit. "And when Paul had laid his hands upon them, the Holy Spirit came on them, and they began speaking with tongues and prophesying." (Acts 19:6)

these multiple functions of tongues to constitute the normative behavior for His church after His ascension to heaven. Paul's first letter to the Corinthian church reveals that the earliest Christians adhered to Jesus' pattern. Paul reveals further insight on the nature of the gift of tongues as prayerful utterance transcending the intellect and subject to the speaker's control.[16] After the biblical era, however, little evidence exists that the pattern established by Jesus and recorded in Paul's writings continued in the church's doctrine and practice. Not only was tongues as the initial evidence of Spirit baptism lost to the body of Christ in early development, but tongues as a gift of the Spirit suffered misunderstanding and disintegration.

After the Apostolic Era
Soon after the apostolic era, the church no longer viewed Spirit baptism as a necessary stage of empowerment to prepare the believer for ministry, but merely co-opted the terminology as another way of speaking about the Spirit's coming at conversion. Spirit baptism was relegated to the convert's experience of receiving the Holy Spirit following the rite of water baptism.[17] The majority of initiates coming

---

[16] Paul's concept, that the speaker in tongues is under voluntary self-control, is identified throughout this chapter as "volitional tongues."
[17] An excellent source for understanding the early church context for charismatic manifestations is *Christian Initiation and Baptism in the Holy Spirit,* by Killian McDonnell and George T. Montague, Collegeville, Minnesota: The Liturgical Press, 1991.

into the church in this early period were adult converts, although infants of church members were also baptized.

Water baptism was the central event of Christian initiation. Following this rite, hands were laid upon the recipient, whether adult or infant, with the expectation of the Spirit's coming. Adults at times would receive manifestations of the Spirit during these occasions. With infants, the church recognized the possibility that spiritual manifestations could occur during a future stage in life. The delay between water baptism and later manifestations, however, did not imply that the manifestation stage was to be viewed as a separate phase of the Spirit's work. The time of manifestation was seen to be an extension of the initial coming of the Spirit. Later manifestations were understood theologically as two parts of one event, i.e., the event of Christian initiation. The notion of a separate, subsequent experience of Spirit baptism for the purpose of ministry empowerment was no longer recognized.

Significance of Tongues Lost
With Spirit baptism no longer viewed as a separate, subsequent experience from conversion, tongues lost its significant function as a sign of initial reception. Tongues became only one of several spiritual manifestations that could occur during the rite of water baptism. For three centuries, spiritual manifestations continued to occur sporadically in local congregations, but tongues was not expected to be integral to the experience of every

Christian. Furthermore, as the bishops of the churches took on added responsibilities and roles formerly shared by the laity, the ministry of the gifts of the Spirit became the exclusive function of church leadership. By the fourth century, in most sectors, even the initiation rite of laying hands upon the newly baptized for Spiritual impartation became purely ritualistic. The vast majority of believers no longer experienced or even expected to be endowed with supernatural power or gifted with supernatural manifestations.

Monastic Preservation

Manifestations of the Spirit never disappeared from Christendom but shifted mostly to the monastic context. Through the Middle Ages and into the Scholastic Era, the Spirit's signs and gifts came to be seen as rewards for extraordinary ascetic discipline, reserved for masters of mystical achievement. Manifestations appeared only in connection with exceptional individuals as "evidence of extreme piety."[18]

The Church Fathers and Beyond

The doctrine and experience of tongues speech gained only limited mention throughout the era of the Church Fathers. Tertullian (160-220) lauded the vitality of the churches under his influence by noting an abundance of Spiritual

---

[18] From the article, "A History of Speaking in Tongues and Related Gifts," by George H. Williams and Edith Waldvogel, *The Charismatic Movement*, ed. Michael P. Hamilton, Grand Rapids, MI: Eerdmans Publishing Company, 1975, p. 71.

manifestations, including the gift of tongues and interpretation of tongues. Novatian (d. 250) spoke of the presence of tongues and other charismata among contemporary churches in his time. Hilary of Poitiers (315-367) defended the orthodoxy of the gifts of tongues and interpretation of tongues in the fourth century. Pachomius (290-346), instrumental in the founding of communal monasticism, on a particular occasion after he had prayed in tongues for three hours, is said to have been able to converse with a visitor in Latin, although he never learned the language.

After a lengthy absence in which the practice of speaking in tongues virtually disappeared from the literature of the church, evidence of the gift reappeared among certain notable monastic figures after the dawning of the next millennium. Hildegard of Bingen (1098-1179), Dominic (1170- 1221), Anthony of Padua (1195-1231) and Clare of Montefalco (1268-1308) are among those who evidenced this gift, although other manifestations of the Spirit such as healing often attracted more attention.

Protestation and Cessationism
With the advent of Protestantism in the sixteenth century, miraculous manifestations were not emphasized. The chief Reformers, Luther, Zwingli and Calvin rejected the legacy of Catholic miracles, particularly as they were used to substantiate the doctrine of the Roman Church. Consequently, Protestantism became identified with the

cessationist theory of miracles. In reaction to Catholic miracles that seemed to be outside Biblical perimeters, most Protestants reasoned that miracles were confined to the New Testament era, when the fledgling Gospel needed supernatural confirmation in order to gain initial acceptance. Protestants placed miracles on the periphery of Christianity, so that they were viewed to be expendable as the Gospel gained a measure of permanence in the world. How ironic it is that the personal experience of Protestantism's founder, Martin Luther, represented an obvious contradiction to the cessationist theory. He sought and received a number of notable healing miracles in the course of his life and ministry. The Protestant movement, however, failed to follow Luther's lead.

George Fox and the Quakers
A significant exception to Protestant cessationism was George Fox (1624-1691), British founder of the Society of Friends. A reactionary movement to the rigid religious uniformity of seventeenth century Anglicanism, the "Quakers" as they were called, viewed miracles to be integral to the intensely personal version of Christianity that they espoused. Fox viewed the wellspring of supernatural manifestations visited upon his ministry as a recovery of the original Pentecost. "...we received often the pouring down of the spirit upon us, and the gift of God's holy eternal spirit as in the days of old, and our hearts were made glad, and our tongues loosed, and our mouths opened, and we spake with new tongues, as the

Lord gave us utterance, and as his spirit led us, which was poured down upon us, on sons and daughters."[19] Fox acknowledged the necessity of the Spirit's empowerment upon his church, and viewed tongues as a sign of this anointing. Other aspects of the doctrine and practice of the Society of Friends lacked Biblical foundations, however, and did not sustain widespread influence. Also, Fox's early emphasis upon supernatural manifestations was not maintained within the Quaker tradition.

The Camisards
Another fringe group kept miracles alive within Protestantism in the eighteenth century. As the persecution of the Protestants in Catholic France resurfaced in the early 1700's, the Huguenots split into two factions. One of those groups, the Camisards (known also as the Prophets of the Cevennes Mountains) claimed to be inspired directly by the Holy Spirit. Ecstatic utterances characterized the movement, and children as well as adults were among the "gifted." Utterances included tongues and interpretation of tongues, although prophetic utterances predominated. Camisards who fled to England were known as French Prophets. Extremist practices surfaced among the French Prophets, as children were organized into strict training programs and instructed in the ways of prophecy. In some instances, children three

---

[19] George Fox, *The Works of George Fox*, Vol. III, New York: AMS Press, 1975 (reprinted from the edition of 1831), p. 13.

years of age and younger were said to have been used for such purposes.

Jesuits and Jansenists

Within Catholicism after the Reformation, evidence of the miraculous continued to be found, mostly in monastic and missionary settings. Jesuit founder Ignatius Loyola (1491-1556) was reported to have received visions that altered the course of his life. His disciple Francis Xavier (1506-1552) was known to have experienced significant miracles as he labored in distant Japan and the West Indies spreading the Jesuit message. Francis depended upon the gift of tongues on several occasions to preach the Gospel to people groups whose language he had never learned. Jansenism, a radical Augustinian movement, sprang up in mid-seventeenth century Catholicism. The papacy dealt severely with this group, whose doctrinal sympathies were judged by Rome to be too Calvinistic. The Jansenists were known for their signs and wonders, spiritual dancing, healings, and prophetic utterances. Some reportedly spoke in tongues.

Wesley and Subsequence

A doctrinal development in eighteenth century English Protestantism contributed by John Wesley (1703-1791) set a precedent for later Pentecostals to advocate that Spirit baptism is a distinct, subsequent experience from conversion. Wesley established the Methodist movement within Anglicanism, an organization that became an independent Protestant denomination after his death. He taught that each Christian should experience a second work of grace beyond conversion, which he identified to be sanctification. Although Wesley emphasized sanctification as a process, spanning the lifetime of the believer, he ventured that this second phase of the Spirit's work often was inaugurated instantaneously.

Successors of the Wesleyan tradition built upon this foundation to introduce a doctrine of subsequence, leading ultimately to the development of Pentecostalism in the American context. Wesley also rejected the cessationist theory typical of Protestantism. He saw no Scriptural basis for the cessation of supernatural gifts of the Spirit, and personally reported an experience of miraculous healing when beset by a serious illness. Yet without question the emphasis of Wesley's doctrine and practice rested on the side of the fruit of the Spirit and the virtures of holiness rather than upon the gifts of the Spirit and supernatural power.

Mother Ann Lee and the Shakers
Mother Ann Lee (1736-1784) and a group of followers relocated from her native England to New York in the American colonies in 1774. The organization that she founded, the Shakers, based their credibility upon direct revelations of the Spirit. Prophetic visions were frequent. Speaking in tongues was integral to the early experience of the movement. Mother Ann not only spoke in tongues but

would write lengthy messages "in the Spirit." A Presbyterian minister who visited revival services in New York in 1779 became convinced that the manifestations that he witnessed were signs of "the baptism of the Spirit." However, questionable doctrines and practices of this fringe movement severely limited its widespread influence in American Christianity.

Edward Irving and the British Revival

Scotsman Edward Irving (1792-1834), a noted London pastor with the Church of Scotland, became convinced that miraculous gifts, signs and wonders of the Holy Spirit had been restored to the church after reports reached him from reliable sources of outbreaks of charismata from the west of Scotland in the summer of 1830. A visitation of similar manifestations within his own congregation led to his dismissal, paving the way for the creation of an independent church pastored by Irving where gifts of the Spirit were welcomed and encouraged. This new congregation founded in 1832, the Newman Street church, became a center for charismatic activity in the London area. Eventually, a London Council of seven churches was formed with Irving as President.

The Catholic Apostolic Church

Irving's untimely death due to illness in 1834 led to significant changes. An apostolic team of leaders raised up at Newman Street assumed control, relocating the headquarters of the movement to rural Albury, south of

London. An international organization was formed under apostolic authority, the Catholic Apostolic Church (CAC). Soon, the new organization evolved into a formalistic, ritualistic entity, vastly different from the spontaneous, charismatic fellowship that once thrived under Irving's leadership at Newman Street.

The New Apostolic Church

Another organization, the New Apostolic Church (NAC), was formed in Germany in the 1860's, as German members of the CAC were excommunicated for appointing their own apostles. The CAC had locked themselves into an apostolic college of only twelve, so that after the last apostle died in 1901, the organization was unable to perpetuate itself. The NAC, with unlimited apostles, expanded internationally during the twentieth century, and continues to be a thriving organization. Although the NAC is less ritualistic than was the CAC, gifts of the Spirit have been relegated to the apostles only. Relevant to our study is the presence of a contemporary organization (the NAC), affirming the authenticity of continuing charismata of the Spirit, tracing its roots back to Edward Irving and the Newman Street church.

Irving's Contributions Not Perpetuated

More important than the groups that were produced by the original movement are the theological formulations contributed by Irving in response to the early outbreak of the charismata. Irving's writings became eclipsed after his death by the preponderance of literary minutia generated by adherents of the CAC. The apostles dramatically altered the character of the CAC from her Newman Street beginnings, and resented being labeled "Irvingite" by outside observers.

The CAC's self-conscious break from Irving's foundational legacy led to the rapid loss of historical memory of Irving's writings related to the charismata. There is a sense in which Christianity has been robbed of invaluable prophetic vision and theological wisdom contributed by a Pentecostal pioneer who forged his way ahead more than seventy years before the appearance of the Pentecostal movement with no guide but the Spirit's illumination and the truths of Scripture. Irving's insights offer biblical, Christological and ecclesiological structure for the proper understanding and expression of the charismata.[20]

---

[20] In *Edward Irving's Holy Spirit Writings*, North Charleston, SC: CreateSpace, 2011, I have edited some of Irving's most important writings covering the outbreak of charismatic gifts and their continuation in his London church, including *The Day of Pentecost or The Baptism with the Holy Ghost*; *On the Gifts of the Holy Ghost, Commonly Called Supernatural;* and *The Church, With Her Endowment of Holiness and Power*. Other publications of mine provide insight regarding Irving's Christological and Pneumatological contributions. David W. Dorries, *Edward Irving's Incarnational Christology*, Fairfax, VA: Xulon Press, 2002; David W. Dorries, "Edward Irving and the 'Standing Sign' of Spirit Baptism," in *Initial Evidence*, ed. Gary B. McGee, Peabody, MA: Hendrickson Publishers, 1991; D. W. Dorries, "West of Scotland Revival (1830)," in *The New International Dictionary of Pentecostal Charismatic Movements*, ed. Stanley M. Burgess, Grand Rapids, MI: Zondervan, 2002.

Irving's Christological Foundations

Irving formulated biblical, Christological foundations for the manifestations of the Spirit. He articulated a doctrine of subsequence, recognizing the Spirit's indwelling of the newly converted believer as being distinct from the event of Spirit baptism, releasing the first fruits of the Spirit's power upon the believer to equip for ministry. First fruits are less than the full harvest of power to be manifested at the time of Jesus' Second Coming but are nonetheless minimally equivalent to the anointing that was upon the incarnate Christ as He ministered the works of the Father in His earthly ministry.

The gift of tongues figured significantly in Irving's scheme, serving as the "standing sign"[21] of Spirit baptism, as well as being "a great instrument for personal edification."[22] The deficiency in Irving's perspective comes in his explanation of the believer's appropriation of the gift of tongues. For Irving, the role of the believer is subsidiary to the Spirit's sovereign choice to bestow the gift. The believer is admonished to desire earnestly the gift, to petition the Father with confidence, and to tarry until the gift is received. Even with the monumental breakthroughs contributed by Edward Irving, his failure to incorporate into his system this Pauline revelation of "volitional tongues" resulted in the restriction of the experience of

---

[21] Edward Irving, ed., David W. Dorries, *Edward Irving's Holy Spirit Writings*, North Charleston, SC: CreateSpace, 2011, p. 140.
[22] Ibid., p. 123.

tongues and Spirit baptism to a limited circle of "gifted" beneficiaries who were privileged to gain the coveted prize.[23] In spite of this major limitation, Irving's Newman Street church came close to recovering for Christendom the Pauline perspective through the influence of experienced leaders such as Emily Cardale and Mary Campbell Caird. Had Irving himself been able to recognize that the reception of Spirit baptism is essentially nothing more than utterances in tongues as a devotional prayer language, to

---

[23] I stand in strong disagreement with Dallimore's basic conclusions regarding the life and ministry of Edward Irving, yet I find his explanation plausible as to the success some of Irving's followers experienced in receiving manifestations, while Irving himself most probably never received tongues, interpretation of tongues, or prophecy. States Dallimore, "It is evident Irving did not want any gift which needed some form of human inducement. The gift of tongues did not come as a direct action from heaven, but means were employed to bring it about. Miss Cardale was considered especially proficient in this regard and made it her practice to say to a seeker, 'Yield your tongue, yield your tongue, yield your tongue to the Holy Ghost!' Likewise, Mary Caird, with her mystical but forceful personality, did much instructing as to how to speak in tongues and was exceptionally successful in the task. Irving condoned these practices, but he wanted something better for himself. He dared not accept any form of the gifts which might leave him with the least doubt as to the supernaturalism of the phenomena... He anticipated the coming on him of 'the power' in what he spoke of as 'a mighty seizure of the Holy Ghost, ...'" Arnold Dallimore, *Forerunner of the Charismatic Movement: The Life of Edward Irving*, Chicago: Moody Press, 1983, pages 134-135. Irving's use of the term "seizure" in reference to the Spirit's coming in Spirit baptism is revealing, for it implies a sovereign imposition of the Spirit upon the recipient leaving no question as to the supernatural origin of the event. He uses the term on another occasion as he describes Mary Campbell's (she became Mary Caird in 1831) initial reception of the gift of tongues. Irving states, "She has told me that this first seizure of the Spirit was the strongest she ever had; ..." *Edward Irving's Holy Spirit Writings*, p. 10.

be exercised as simply and freely as the practice of praying regularly in one's understanding, his movement possibly could have catapulted itself out of obscurity into a place of precipitating a major Pentecostal revival ahead of the Azusa Street phenomenon.

Phoebe Palmer and American Methodism

Turning to the American context in the nineteenth century, a Methodist woman named Phoebe Palmer devoted more than forty years of her life to an influential teaching ministry aimed at encouraging Methodists to receive sanctification through an instantaneous experience that she identified to be the baptism of the Holy Spirit. She utilized Pentecostal language to characterize this crisis experience of perfect holiness possible for the believer. The gift of tongues and other charismata, however, were not integrated into her agenda.

The Holiness Movement

By the 1860's, a Holiness movement materialized within Methodism, advocating sanctification as a distinct experience for believers, and promoting revivals within the churches. "Higher life" conferences in Keswick, England in the late nineteenth century paralleled the American emphasis upon holiness as a distinct work of grace in Christian experience. As Holiness advocates within Methodism became disillusioned with denominational resistance to their emphasis upon sanctification as an experiential priority, a "come-outer" movement during the 1890's swept through Methodism as hundreds of Holiness devotees abandoned their institutional affiliation to form various independent holiness organizations around the country. Out of this milieu, sympathetic to multiple works of grace, crisis experiences and revivalism, Pentecostalism would be born.

Benjamin Irwin and the Fire-Baptized Holiness Church

A former Baptist minister, B. H. Irwin, successfully organized Holiness groups into a denomination that swept through the Midwest, becoming known as the Fire-baptized Holiness Church (1895). Irwin concluded that a third experience beyond sanctification was possible for believers. Challenging Palmer's theory, Irwin contended that the third and not the second experience was "the baptism with the Holy Ghost and fire" or just "the fire." No specific sign indicated to the recipient that "the fire" had been obtained. As Spirit baptism was received, any number of manifestations could occur: screaming, shouting, falling into trances, speaking in tongues, or experiencing "the jerks." By 1900, Irwin was not content with three works of grace. He concluded that additional baptisms are necessary for the perfection of the Christian. He employed chemical jargon in the naming of these successive baptisms: dynamite, lyddite and oxidite. A seventh baptism was added (celenite). Most members of the group, however, never accepted these progressive stages of perfection. A moral failure brought to light in 1900 led to the departure of Irwin as overseer of the denomination, and the organization never regained its original influence.

Charles Parham and Spirit Baptism

Charles Parham was a former Methodist minister who became independent after 1895 as the "come-outer" movement impacted Methodism. From his Methodist background, Parham accepted the teaching that sanctification was a second work of grace beyond conversion and was influenced additionally by Irwin that a third work of grace was desirable. Located in Topeka, Kansas, Parham began the Bethel Healing Home (1898) and the Bethel Bible School (1900). Late in 1900, Parham and his students reached the conclusion that the Scriptural evidence for determining that one had received the baptism in the Spirit is speaking in tongues. As the school conducted a watchnight service on December 31, 1900, a service extending into the New Year, student Agnes Ozman requested prayer from Parham to receive Spirit baptism. Her experience of speaking in tongues was so captivating that she continued at length in prayer, unable to communicate in her own language for three days. Parham and other students also received the evidence of speaking in tongues. Convinced that his teaching represented the recovery of the upper room experience on the Day of Pentecost, Parham closed the school and took his ministry on the road.

The Emergence of William Seymour

Twentieth century Pentecostals recognize Parham as being the father of the "classical Pentecostal doctrine" helping to ignite the modern Pentecostal movement. Yet his message failed to gain acceptance initially. For four years, he and his group labored in obscurity. In 1905, he found enough support in Houston, Texas to locate his headquarters there. He founded another school in Houston, "The Bible Training School." Parham's decision to teach was significant, for one of the enrollees in his school was William J. Seymour. Seymour was a black evangelist from Louisiana, desirous of receiving biblical training from Parham. Seymour eagerly adopted Parham's Pentecostal teaching. Already convinced that sanctification was a second work of grace, Seymour now embraced Spirit baptism as a third blessing for the believer's empowerment, evidenced by the experience of speaking in tongues.

Los Angeles Stirrings

In the winter of 1906, Seymour was contacted by members of a storefront Holiness congregation in Los Angeles, California, recruiting him to be their pastor. Seymour accepted, and journeyed by train to assume his new position. Seymour preached only a few sermons but found himself locked out of the building of his new pastorate. Members were not prepared to accept Seymour's doctrine of Spirit baptism. Even though Seymour had not yet received the experience, his preaching emphasis upon speaking in tongues alienated his hearers.

The Azusa Street Revival

Without a job or a home of his own, Seymour was given temporary shelter and dedicated himself to a season of intense prayer. Eventually, a family took him in and persuaded him to offer services in their home. The tide turned in favor of Seymour and his message, and crowds flocked to the home meetings. Interest was so high that a former church building was secured at 312 Azusa Street. Calling themselves the Apostolic Faith Mission, the group began services in April under Seymour's pastoral leadership. The opening of the mission coincided with a stirring revival among the core members of the new church. Seymour and others received the baptism in the Holy Spirit. The Los Angeles media publicized the Azusa Street events. Attendance mushroomed, and revival broke out in the services. Seymour printed a newsletter highlighting the Pentecostal outpouring, and news spread to Holiness denominations throughout America. Revival flourished to the extent that services at times at Azusa Street became consecutive, continuing without interruption, night and day. Pentecostal missionaries from Azusa Street spread the message of Spirit baptism around the world. Revival was unbroken for three years (1906-1909). The Azusa Street revival spawned a worldwide Pentecostal movement whose influence has continued into the twenty-first century.

Forgotten Azusa Street Factors

Several factors that contributed to revival at Azusa Street were not perpetuated within the Pentecostal movement that followed the initial revival. The humble circumstances of the mission encouraged people from all races, classes and cultural backgrounds to feel on equal footing at Azusa Street. Seymour recognized that the true foundation for the revival was the presence of interracial, intercultural unity, providing an atmosphere of humility and brokenness among the people that invited the Spirit's presence and Pentecostal power. In addition, Seymour was an exceptionally humble leader, willing to be a background figure courageous enough to allow the Holy Spirit to move freely without hindrance. Seymour's integrity and willingness to give room for the sovereign move of the Spirit, as well as the interracial unity of Azusa Street, were factors characteristic of the early phase of revival that were lost sight of as the Pentecostal movement began to take root.

Factors Carried into the Pentecostal Movement

On the other hand, the manifestation and magnification of the doctrine of Spirit baptism, with the accompanying reaffirmation of the New Testament practice of speaking in tongues as the initial sign of this subsequent blessing of Christian empowerment, was a positive factor from Azusa Street that was disseminated and institutionalized within the Pentecostal movement. The fact that some Pentecostal denominations accepted sanctification as a second work of grace, as in the cases of Parham and Seymour, while others viewed sanctification as a part of the conversion experience, thus rendering Spirit baptism as a second rather than a third distinct Christian experience, proved to be only a minor difference among the throng of Pentecostals that were establishing their permanent place within the worldwide community of Christians.

Pentecostal Denominations
As Pentecostal denominationalism passed the baton to the next generation, dynamic features of Pentecostalism experienced a measure of ossification. Denominations maintained the concept of subsequence for Spirit baptism, and insisted upon tongues as the initial sign, but spontaneity of experience gave way to structured worship and formality. Pentecostals yielded to pressures to conform to mainstream Christian practices, which brought increased acceptability within society, but resulted in a de-emphasis of Pentecostal distinctives. We must note, however, that the positive consequence of Pentecostal acceptability meant that this new movement had earned a place within the landscape of Christendom that could not be ignored.

"Volitional Tongues" Not Yet Recovered
Both the Azusa Street revival and the Pentecostal denominations brought prominence to Spirit baptism and tongues as the initial sign of reception, while failing to

recover the Pauline emphasis upon "volitional tongues." We remember that Irving's Newman Street church had established the value of tongues as a language of prayer, available to every believer, but had not provided a viable means for implementing tongues for everyone. Consequently, only a select group actually received tongues, forming an elite group of the "gifted" who had attained preferential status within the church. Even Irving, whose teaching on tongues as a gift has yet to be exceeded, did not find himself among the "gifted" few.

Seymour and Azusa Street proved to be more successful in the ministry of implementation, in their focus upon the empirical verifiability of Spirit baptism by means of the tongues experience. This focus was transmitted into the Pentecostal movement. Yet with the gains of Pentecostalism, the outcome fell short of restoring Paul's "volitional tongues." Pentecostalism maintained the "tarrying" facet of receiving tongues,[24] meaning that the desire for tongues must be matched by the appropriate timing and subjective feeling for satisfactory appropriation to take place. While many would conclude the process having attained a successful outcome, others mystifyingly would fail to gain the coveted prize.

---

[24] This was a carryover from the "camp meeting" format common to the American Methodist background familiar to early Pentecostals. Responding to an "altar call," potential recipients of various experiences knelt at the altar to tarry for an expected spiritual outcome.

The Charismatic Movement

New dynamics dominated the scene as the Charismatic movement came into prominence in the 1960's. The Charismatic movement flooded both Protestantism and Catholicism, and to a lesser extent, Eastern Orthodoxy, with a fresh wave of Pentecostal awareness and experience. Renewal groups sprang up within mainline Christian denominations, providing validation and encouragement for the experience of Spirit baptism as a distinctive work of the Holy Spirit. Innovation marked the Charismatic movement, in that tongues was no longer seen by some to be the necessary sign of Spirit baptism, but only one among other possible manifestations that could characterize the reception of this distinctive blessing. Most groups preferred tongues as the initial sign, but the door was opened for believers to claim possession of the experience without having spoken in tongues.

Charismatics Receptive to "Volitional Tongues"

Despite this innovation, the Charismatic movement contributed a breakthrough on a major scale that other previous groups sympathetic to Pentecostalism had failed to provide. "Volitional tongues" became a prominent teaching within various Charismatic and independent circles, recovering a basic practice common to New Testament Christianity in the days of the apostle Paul but soon abandoned by the churches. Research has not yet uncovered the source or sources within the pre-Charismatic milieu responsible for reintroducing "volitional tongues" as a Pentecostal truth. The teaching surfaced probably in the 1940's, possibly through the ministry of Smith Wigglesworth and possibly in the Latter Rain revival that began in Canada in 1948. Pentecostal leaders who were contemporaries of the Charismatic movement and were prominent advocates of the "volitional tongues" perspective were Oral Roberts, David du Plessis, Demos Shakarian, Pat Robertson and Kenneth Hagin, among others. Yet regardless of the initiating agent or agents fostering widespread acceptance of this teaching, it is undeniable that the Charismatic movement was responsible for preparing the way for an unprecedented number of initiates to receive the manifestation of speaking in tongues throughout the world, spanning every Christian denomination.

Value of Volitional Tongues
Among the practical consequences of the widespread acceptance of "volitional tongues" promoted by the Charismatic movement are the demystification and desubjectification of the experience. Armed with the knowledge that speaking in tongues may be commenced at will, the believer will tend to experience Spirit baptism more quickly without waiting for a special timing or feeling. Once baptized in the Spirit, believers will more frequently practice tongues as a regular language of prayer, realizing that the original experience was simply one of numerous experiences of personal empowerment meant to continually build up the believer for Christian

living. The Holy Spirit is always ready to stir the human spirit to pray in the heavenly language of tongues. The responsibility rests with the believer to vocalize those utterances that flow from deep within the human spirit through the urging of the Holy Spirit.

A Truth for All Christians

The Charismatic movement became a vehicle for awakening the church to a truth of New Testament experience that for centuries has been forgotten by Christendom. The teaching of "volitional tongues," while being a Charismatic distinctive, is, more importantly, a biblical, New Testament distinctive. A truth revealed to the church through Paul, this teaching was meant to be believed and implemented by all Christians. The human spirit was created to engage in continuous communion with the indwelling Holy Spirit, and the expression of tongues is a primary means of maintaining intimacy with Jesus and experiencing His ministry in continuous relationship.

The Pauline Context

Perhaps the radical implications of this teaching can be highlighted more clearly if the primary Scriptural text from Paul's writing is accentuated. Paul articulates the nature and proper expression of the gift of tongues in I Corinthians 14. More is said in this chapter about speaking in tongues than anywhere else in the New Testament. In this context, a paraphrase of key verses in this chapter specifically focusing upon tongues is ventured, in expectation that readers will grasp Paul's mindset in a fresh way, bringing enhanced insight and vision of this invaluable truth.

I Corinthians 14

"When the believer is speaking in tongues, he is not speaking to men but to God. He is speaking mysteries to God flowing out of his human spirit. (2) When one is speaking in tongues, he is being edified and built up in his faith. (4) Therefore, I wish that all of you would enter into the practice of speaking in tongues. (5) Speaking in tongues is a form of prayer, yet not a conceptual expression of the intellect, but a prayer originating from the human spirit. (14) Just as the believer chooses to pray or sing to God with intellectual comprehension, so should the believer choose to pray and sing to God in tongues. Yet when believers are gathered together in worship, consideration must be made for the good of the assembly. Even though I am thankful that I speak in tongues privately more than all of you, I control myself when I am worshipping with others. In the assembly, five words that can be understood are better than ten thousand words spoken in tongues. (18-19) During worship, it is best for only two or three of you to bring a message in tongues, and only when one is present to interpret each message through the gift of interpretation. Otherwise, it is better to refrain from speaking in tongues in the assembly, but to continue to pray in tongues in your private devotions to God." (27-28)

Third Wave Neo-charismatics

An extension of the Charismatic movement has been the emergence of what has been labeled the "Third Wave" of Pentecostalism (Neo-charismatics). The Charismatics sought to bring renewal in the Holy Spirit to denominational Christianity. Neo-charismatics established their identity outside structures of the denominational church. Within Protestantism, Third Wave groups proliferated by the thousands. While most of these groups remained small and limited in influence, others developed highly organized entities similar to major corporations, with branches extending in some cases even beyond national borders. Neo-charismatics have been responsible for spawning "mega-churches" and "mini-denominations" significantly impacting worldwide Christianity. Many of the largest churches in the world today have been produced by the Third Wave movement originating out of the Charismatic movement. In addition, thousands of para-church ministries that are Charismatic in orientation, but not denominationally related, have found their place in Christendom as a result of the Third Wave movement.

Contemporary Independents

These independent Neo-charismatics in the modern world are a force to be reckoned with. Some operate with a "corporate" infrastructure, supporting hundreds of affiliate churches and ministries. Some are loosely assembled, while others are maintained by authoritarian government under singular or group leadership. An "apostolic" movement is thriving within this milieu, as churches have ordered themselves under the leadership of apostles in an effort to recover this New Testament pattern. In line with the focus of this chapter, we have observed general continuity in belief and practice with the Charismatic movement. Many of the independents view Spirit baptism as a distinct experience subsequent to conversion for the basic purpose of equipping the believer with the supernatural power of the Spirit. When compared with the original Charismatics, attempting to influence mainline denominations with the Spirit's gifts, signs and wonders, the independents are more insistent in their belief that speaking in tongues is the initial sign of the baptism in the Holy Spirit. They are less likely to compromise this tenet of "classical Pentecostalism." In addition, they have perpetuated the Charismatic recovery of "volitional tongues," thereby fostering the concept that tongues should be a frequent, normal practice in the devotional life of every Christian.

Chapter 12

Conclusion

A NEW DIMENSION OF CHRISTIAN LIVING emerges when we discover that Jesus was fully human, and the fruit and gifts of the Spirit that characterized His earthly life are available to every Christian. Even more amazing is the reality that we are not on our own, futilely striving to imitate His lifestyle. Jesus as the Risen Lord comes to dwell in the life of every believer, permeating our mind, emotions and will with His living presence. We can dispense once and for all with the religious notion that we are obligated to perform, serve or do something for God. If we have created in our self-perception a distance between ourselves and God, i.e., that God is in heaven watching our behavior, then we have departed from the truth of the Gospel.

Jesus' parable of the vine and the branches is a vivid portrayal of the Christian life. The living presence of Jesus flows from the vine into the branches, making possible the production of fruit. The branch can never produce fruit if it is detached from the vine. As Jesus explained, "I am the vine, you are the branches; he who abides in Me and I in him, he bears much fruit, for apart from Me you can do nothing." (John 15:5) We don't perform for God. We allow Him to perform His will in and through us. Far from independently taking control of our life and trying to live for Him, we learn the art of discerning His presence within us and yielding to His promptings to think, say and act according to His direction. We are not puppets being manipulated against our will. We are fully engaged in tuning in to His presence and guidance.

The Presence of Divinity that Empowered Jesus was the Holy Spirit

The Holy Spirit indwelt and filled Jesus' human life, so that divine, supernatural presence and capacity was always with Him. Jesus never attempted to step outside the boundaries of His weak and frail humanity in the accomplishment of mighty miracles. Yet supernatural power flowed from His humanity, because He remained dependent upon the Holy Spirit, the source of His power. That the presence of divinity within Jesus' humanity was the Holy Spirit, and not His own divine nature as God's Son, is a matter of immense doctrinal significance. (John

3:34-35, Isaiah 42:1, Matthew 12:15-18, Isaiah 61:1, Luke 4:16-21)

The divinity that He expressed was not His inherent divinity as the Word and Son but had its source from another member of the Triune Godhead. Jesus' role as a model of desired human behavior has validity because the source of divine agency within Him, prompting and empowering Him to do the Father's works, is the Holy Spirit. "You know of Jesus of Nazareth, how God anointed Him with the Holy Spirit and with power, ..." (Acts 10:38) "And Jesus, full of the Holy Spirit, ...was led about by the Spirit ...And Jesus returned to Galilee in the power of the Spirit; ..." (Luke 4:1, 14) "But if I cast out demons by the Spirit of God, then the kingdom of God has come upon you." (Matthew 12:28)

Even the Miracles of Jesus were through the Spirit's Anointing

Christian opinion for too long has falsely hoisted Jesus on a pedestal by attributing the miracles that He performed to His divine majesty. Although Jesus deserves our praise for His legacy of miraculous works, we are not detracting from the praise for which He is due because we recognize that His miracles were accomplished through the Spirit's anointing upon Him. That He ministered so powerfully without relying upon the resources of His own divine nature is an accomplishment of far greater magnitude than had He insisted upon utilizing His divinity.

By doing miraculous works in the weakness of His humanity, while depending upon the Spirit's power, Jesus was demonstrating to His disciples how His supernatural ministry should be continued when He would no longer be physically present. If Jesus depended upon the Spirit to do miraculous works, so can we. "And He has said to me, 'My grace is sufficient for you, for power is perfected in weakness.' Most gladly, therefore, I will rather boast about my weaknesses, that the power of Christ may dwell in me. ...for when I am weak, then I am strong." (II Corinthians 12:9-10)

Had Jesus activated the attributes of His divine nature during His incarnate mission, whether in resisting temptation or in working miracles, He would have violated the standards of redemption set by His Father. (Matthew 27:42, Luke 22:42) It is not consistent with the nature of humanity to manifest divine attributes. To admit belief in the Incarnation, while contending that Jesus manifested attributes of His divine nature, represents logical contradiction. The Incarnation of the Son of God is an essential biblical reality. Therefore, the inactivity of Jesus' divine attributes during His redemptive mission is a necessary consequence of His Incarnation and represents the only logical conclusion that preserves Jesus' essential divinity and His authentic humanity.

Redemption is a Free Gift

After His resurrection from the dead, Jesus rose as the Redeemer for all humanity. His act of breathing upon His disciples to receive the Holy Spirit represented the inauguration of the new birth within human history. (John 20:19-22) Collectively, His new born disciples were constituted as the first members of the Christian church. Jesus' breath of regenerative life upon those disciples signifies the birthday of the church. From this point forward, all members of the human race willing to receive Jesus as the resurrected Redeemer may become sons and daughters of God, and members of the church. "But as many as received Him, to them He gave the right to become children of God, even to those who believe in His name, ..." (John 1:12) The faith to receive Jesus and His salvation must never be considered a work on our part, something done to earn our salvation. That would leave room on our part for boasting that we had contributed to our own salvation. Paul approves of boasting only in God, whose graciousness solely is responsible for our salvation. Human works can neither add nor take away from the finished work of Jesus Christ on the cross. Justification is based solely upon the victory that was finished on the cross, and it is actualized in the individual simply by believing in the accomplishment of Jesus.

The Resurrected Christ Continues to Live and Work through His Church

Jesus' presence, blessings and power are not external goals to be acquired by superior spiritual performance but are freely bestowed giftings that accompany Christ's presence. The Spirit does not respond to the believer's works but leads the believer to respond to the works of Christ in His continuing mission in the earth. "But when He, the Spirit of truth, comes, He will guide you into all the truth; for He will not speak on His own initiative, but whatever He hears, He will speak; and He will disclose to you what is to come. He will glorify Me, for He will take of Mine and will disclose it to you. All things that the Father has are Mine; therefore I said that He takes of Mine and will disclose it to you." (John 16:13-15)

When Christians are found to be trying to impress God, to measure up, to do something for God, or to obtain the blessings of the abundant life by spiritual performances, they are displaying symptoms of immature, fleshly behavior. Christians do not live for Jesus, but rather, have died to self-life and have become vessels of the indwelling Christ through the Spirit's presence.

We have trouble really believing that our Gospel is a Gospel of grace. Rather than gratefully receiving Jesus Christ and the full endowment of giftings and benefits associated with His baptism in the Spirit, we are tempted to fall back into carnality by attempting to do something for God to reciprocate for our good fortune. "But if it is by grace, it is no longer on the basis of works, otherwise grace is no longer grace." (Romans 11:6)

Fulfilling the Church's Commission Requires Spirit Baptism

Becoming new born believers carries with it the responsibility of abiding in Jesus (John 15:4) and contributing to the task of the Great Commission He assigned to the church prior to His ascension. The church has been commissioned by Jesus to make new disciples, and to transmit His Gospel to the uttermost parts of the world. (Matthew 28:19-20, Mark 16:15-16) Jesus required that His church receive the Holy Spirit's baptism of empowerment before venturing out to begin the implementation of His Commission. "And behold, I am sending forth the promise of My Father upon you; but you are to stay in the city until you are clothed with power from on high." (Luke 24:49) "...He commanded them not to leave Jerusalem, but to wait for what the Father had promised, ...for John baptized with water, but you shall be baptized with the Holy Spirit not many days from now." (Acts 1:4-5)

Jesus is Baptizer in the Holy Spirit

Following His ascension, Jesus assumed His role as Baptizer in the Holy Spirit. "He will baptize you with the Holy Spirit and fire." (Matthew 3:11) On the Day of Pentecost, He baptized His church with power from on high, enabling them to confirm the proclamation of the Gospel with signs, wonders and miracles following. "Therefore, having been exalted to the right hand of God and having received from the Father the promise of the

Holy Spirit, He has poured forth this which you both see and hear." (Acts 2:33) The same Jesus who stepped into His role as Baptizer of the Holy Spirit on the Day of Pentecost is the One who received and depended upon the Holy Spirit in His incarnate humanity. Giver of the Holy Spirit as God, Jesus also received the Holy Spirit when He became human for the sake of human redemption. Since the Day of Pentecost, the baptism of the Holy Spirit has been available for all new born believers, representing a subsequent experience of power following conversion. (Acts 2:38-39)

Although Spirit baptism may be received in chronological simultaneity with the new birth, nonetheless logically it should always remain a distinct experience from conversion. The Holy Spirit comes to indwell the believer at conversion, bringing forgiveness and regeneration. In Spirit baptism, the Holy Spirit equips supernaturally the regenerated believer with gifts, signs and wonders for the expressed purpose of carrying out Jesus' Commission. "…but you shall receive power when the Holy Spirit has come upon you; and you shall be My witnesses both in Jerusalem, and in all Judea and Samaria, and even to the remotest part of the earth." (Acts 1:8)

Speaking in Tongues
Reception of Spirit baptism is evidenced by speaking in unknown tongues, as was typical in the Book of Acts. "And they were all filled with the Holy Spirit and began to

speak with other tongues, as the Spirit was giving them utterance." (Acts 2:4) Speaking in tongues is foremost a language of prayer and may be spoken at will as a prayerful and empowering form of communication with God the Father. "For one who speaks in a tongue does not speak to men, but to God; ..." (I Corinthians 14:2) The human spirit was created to engage in continuous communion with the indwelling Holy Spirit, and the expression of tongues is a primary means of maintaining intimacy with Jesus and experiencing His ministry in continuous relationship. "...in his spirit he speaks mysteries." (I Corinthians 14:2) Secondarily, it is a gift to be expressed in an orderly fashion among believers when an interpreter of tongues is present. (I Corinthians 14:27-28)

Like praying in the language of one's understanding, praying in the language of the Spirit is a controlled action free to occur whenever the speaker is willing. "What is the outcome then? I shall pray with the spirit and I shall pray with the mind also; I shall sing with the spirit and I shall sing with the mind also." (I Corinthians 14:15) When contemporary Christianity rediscovers and implements the biblical pattern concerning Jesus as Baptizer in the Holy Spirit and the Pauline revelation concerning speaking in tongues, revival will ignite the church with lasting reformation looming on the horizon.

We have seen that tongues is a form of prayer. More specifically, tongues is an expression of worship so utterly pure and primordial that its meaning transcends conceptual comprehension. "For if I pray in a tongue, my spirit prays, but my mind is unfruitful." (I Corinthians 14:14) As the speaker yields consent to voice this deep form of praise to God, the indwelling Holy Spirit infuses the entire being of the speaker with supernatural power. "One who speaks in a tongue edifies himself; ..." (I Corinthians 14:4) The utterances are spoken as an act of faith, a total surrender of the voice and tongue to syllables unknown to the intellect. The pride of human intelligence must bow in submission to incomprehensible babblings believed to be the humble articulations of a completely yielded vessel.

Jesus Demonstrated Spirit-filled Living
Jesus' lived an authentically human life in complete dependence upon the Holy Spirit. He exemplified a life of consistent faith in His Father's provision through the Spirit. Weak in His humanity, He was strong in faith. "In the days of His flesh, when He offered up both prayers and supplications with loud crying and tears to Him who was able to save Him from death, and who was heard because of His piety, ..." (Hebrews 5:7) This life of complete dependence not only enabled Him to meet the requirements for redemption, but also served to demonstrate in His own life the pattern of Spirit-filled living He intends for believers to follow. Jesus' holiness

was through moral obedience in dependence upon the sanctifying presence of the Holy Spirit, not through the inherent holiness of His divine nature. By intention, He set a pattern for sanctified living for all believers, in that the Holy Spirit is present in all believers to produce sanctification in union with His holy humanity. "For since He Himself was tempted in that which He has suffered, He is able to come to the aid of those who are tempted." (Hebrews 2:18)

The personal mission and destiny of the life of the individual believer can be achieved only as the Holy Spirit is given freedom to enforce the Lordship of Jesus in every facet of thought and action. Jesus purposefully did not activate the supernatural attributes of His divine nature and depended upon the Spirit's power in the living out of His miraculous ministry. He desires for His church, through the experience of Spirit baptism, to work the same and even greater works than did He in the exercise of His public ministry. The same Holy Spirit that empowered Jesus is available to empower His church in the world today.

Jesus lived out His incarnate life with this purpose in mind. He intended for His human existence to be a pattern for His church of what it means to live life in complete submission and compliance with the operations of the Holy Spirit. This is true, both in sanctification and in empowerment. Had Jesus' done the Father's works through dependence upon His inherent divinity, then He would not have qualified to be our example. We do not, nor will we ever, have a divine nature to be the source of our words and works. But if the same Holy Spirit provided by the Father for Jesus to rely upon is also provided for us, then the possibility now exists for Jesus to be our example. "…as He is, so also are we in this world." (I John 4:17) "…the one who says he abides in Him ought himself to walk in the same manner as He walked." (I John 2:6) "For you have been called for this purpose, since Christ also suffered for you, leaving you an example for you to follow in His steps." (I Peter 2:21)

Jesus' Anointing is also Ours

It is futile to attempt to follow the example of Jesus' lifestyle without having first received Him as gift. Humanity devoid of the Holy Spirit is powerless to emulate the lifestyle Jesus modeled. The baptism of the Spirit imparted by Jesus upon the early church was never rescinded but represents a continuous reservoir of spiritual life and power available to every generation of believers who will partake. Jesus never intended His Gospel to be transmitted in word only but conveyed to a needy world in demonstration of the Spirit and power. "And my message and my preaching were not in persuasive words of wisdom, but in demonstration of the Spirit and of power, so that your faith would not rest on the wisdom of men, but on the power of God." (I Corinthians 2:4-5) "For the kingdom of God does not consist in words, but in power." (I Corinthians 4:20) When He imparted the Holy Spirit unto every believer, He endowed them with the same sanctifying presence that enabled Him to resist sin and live with a pure conscience before the Father. When He poured out from heaven the Pentecostal baptism of the Holy Spirit, He equipped His church with the same supernatural anointing that characterized His public ministry. "And as for you, the anointing which you received from Him abides in you, ..." (I John 2:27)

If Christians view Jesus' supernatural works as setting a pattern for what the church is to accomplish, then faith is increased within the church to follow through with the challenge of the Great Commission. "These signs will accompany those who have believed: in My name they will cast out demons, they will speak with new tongues; they will pick up serpents, and if they drink any deadly poison, it will not hurt them; they will lay hands on the sick, and they will recover." (Mark 16:17-18) Incentive is diminished when believers face a daunting assignment with no confidence that supernatural assistance is available. To applaud Jesus for His supernatural ministry, while believing that we are powerless to do similar works, affords Him no glory.

Jesus' taught His disciples to expect a lifestyle of the Spirit's anointing. Jesus fully intended that His life of sanctification and power be reproduced by those coming after Him, for the Spirit that filled His humanity would also fill them. "But you have an anointing from the Holy One, and you all know." (I John 2:20) Our role is not to imitate Jesus' actions as we remember His deeds, but to participate with Him as He continues to minister to people in the mighty power of the Spirit. "And they went out and preached everywhere, while the Lord worked with them, and confirmed the word by the signs that followed." (Mark 16:20) Willing vessels free to be used are those submitted to the baptism of the Holy Spirit. No more glorious occupation has ever graced God's children than to be habitations of the Holy Spirit.

APPENDIX I

HOW TO RECEIVE JESUS AS YOUR PERSONAL SAVIOR

"But as many as received Him, to them He gave the right to become the children of God, even to those who believe in His name, ..." (John 1:12)

THE GOSPEL IS NOT about what we must do to acquire Jesus and His salvation. The Gospel is about what Jesus did to provide salvation for the human race, freely and without condition.

Change in our lives comes only after we receive Jesus, not before. Only when He has been invited to come in does the process of change begin. The Holy Spirit accompanies Jesus and makes change possible. Receiving Jesus only requires that we come empty handed, as sinners. We come, willing to receive Jesus as a gift. We know that we have not earned, nor do we deserve, the salvation Jesus provides. We come, as needy people, willing to receive.

"For by grace you have been saved through faith; and that not of yourselves, it is the gift of God; not as a result of works, so that no one may boast." (Ephesians 2:8-9)

No one is excluded from the offer of salvation through Jesus Christ. Jesus was not ashamed to become human. He lived a life of complete human obedience and gave Himself up to death on the cross for our sakes. What He did for humanity applies for every member of the human race.

"He Himself is the propitiation (appeasement, satisfaction) for our sins; and not for ours only, but also for those of the whole world." (I John 2:2)

Pray this prayer to God now, with sincerity, and Jesus gladly will come to dwell in you permanently as your Savior and Lord.

"Dear Father God, thank you for Jesus, and for His life, death and resurrection for my sake. I come to You as a sinner, not worthy of Your salvation. I ask for Jesus to come into my life at this very moment through the Holy Spirit. I receive forgiveness for all my sins, and I accept a new beginning in life with Jesus as my Lord. Father, now

I know that I am a new born believer. I know that I now have life, abundant and eternal. Guide and control my life, from this day forward. Amen!

APPENDIX II

HOW TO RECEIVE THE BAPTISM OF THE HOLY SPIRIT

WHEN JESUS BAPTIZED His disciples in the Holy Spirit on the Day of Pentecost, He was making Spirit baptism available for all Christians for all times. In fact, He requires that all Christians receive this *"power from on high"* (Luke 24:49) before trying to carry out His work. The best of human strength is woefully inadequate to fulfill the purposes of Jesus Christ in the earth. We need the supernatural resources of Spirit baptism in order to implement the will of God.

Our confidence that we have received the baptism of the Holy Spirit is the experience of speaking in tongues. Since it is a form of prayer, it is an utterance that the believer is able to control. When Spirit baptism was first released by

Jesus upon His disciples, **they** *"began to speak with other tongues, as the Spirit was giving them utterance."* (Acts 2:4) Notice that the believers did the speaking, not the Holy Spirit. Some people have the idea that speaking in tongues is like a spiritual trance beyond the control of the speaker. That idea is not biblical. Paul taught that speaking in tongues is a voluntary practice. *"...I will pray with the spirit ...and I will sing with the spirit ..."* (I Corinthians 14:15 NKJV) He instructed believers not to speak in tongues in the assembly when an interpreter is not present. In that instance, it is better to "keep silent in the church; and let him speak to himself and to God." (I Corinthians 14:28) This implies that tongues speech is able to be controlled. Viewing speaking in tongues as a frenzied activity performed in a trance-like state is the stuff of pagan religions, not the biblical practice of tongues speech in Christian experience.

Like prayer, speaking in tongues is meant for every Christian, because it is a means for the believer to experience inner communion with the Holy Spirit. This practice ushers the believer into the supernatural realm of the Spirit's power. The believer is built up in the Spirit's strength and becomes available to operate in other gifts of the Holy Spirit. God does not show partiality. He would not allow these privileges to a few of His children, while depriving others. Paul made the appeal to all Christians when he said, *"I wish that you all spoke in tongues, ..."* (I

Corinthians 14:5) Spirit baptism has been released upon the church and continues to be available to all.

For anyone desiring to receive the baptism of the Spirit, keep in mind that praying in tongues soon will become as simple for you as praying to God in your own understanding. Your first step is to ask Father God to baptize you in the Holy Spirit. Begin thanking and praising Him, but do not allow yourself to speak in your own language or any known language. Speak only in "syllables of faith."[25] Begin exercising your vocal chords. Allow sounds to be vocalized, without expecting to understand what you are saying. While speaking these unknown utterances, force yourself to stop. Then start up again. This will assure you that you have chosen to speak in tongues, and can do so at will, anytime.

Focus upon Jesus as you allow your new tongues to flow. You are now baptized in the Holy Spirit! Speak in tongues freely and frequently. You will find yourself more receptive to the things of God. Be open to receiving other gifts of the Spirit (I Corinthians 12:8-10) You will never be the same!

---

[25] I first heard the phrase, "syllables of faith," from Pastor David Ingles of Walnut Grove Church in Broken Arrow, Oklahoma. His ministry in leading persons to receive Spirit baptism is one of the most effective I have had the privilege of witnessing.

Made in the USA
Columbia, SC
20 June 2018